Ekkehard Spann

Zentrale Klassenarbeit Baden-Württemberg

Englisch 10. Schuljahr

MANZ VERLAG

9. Auflage 2007
Manz Verlag

Lektorat: Harald Kotlarz, Rottenburg
Herstellung: imprint, Zusmarshausen
Umschlagkonzept: KünkelLopka, Heidelberg
Umschlagfoto: Fotostudio Maurer, Bamberg
Druck: Finidr s.r.o., Český Těšín

ISBN: 978-3-7863-2058-6

www.manz-verlag.de

Inhaltsverzeichnis

Einführung

Die Zentrale Klassenarbeit

Um was geht es?

Die Zentrale Klassenarbeit in Baden-Württemberg wird zum Abschluss der zehnten Klasse zentral gestellt und findet an einem Haupttermin im Mai/Juni statt.
Für Nachzügler wird noch ein Nachtermin angeboten. Sie setzt sich aus einer Hörverstehensaufgabe mit drei Fragen, einem *comment* und einer Übersetzung zusammen.

Sie wird doppelt gezählt, entspricht also **zwei Klassenarbeiten**.

Sie wird von 8.00 Uhr bis 9.30 Uhr geschrieben. Für den Teil A, die „Erweiterte Hörverstehensaufgabe", stehen 50 Minuten zur Verfügung, für die Übersetzung 40 Minuten. 50 Minuten nach Beginn der Arbeit wird der Text für die Übersetzung ausgegeben. Nach 90 Minuten werden beide Teile eingesammelt.

Durchführung Teil A – Erweiterte Hörverstehensaufgabe

1. Die Wortangaben werden angeschrieben und vorgelesen. Die Erklärungen können ein- oder zweisprachig sein.
2. Der Text wird das erste Mal vorgelesen (Notizen sind dabei nicht erlaubt).
3. Nach dem ersten Vorlesen wird das Aufgabenblatt ausgeteilt.
   Es enthält drei Fragen zum Text und das Thema für den *comment*.
4. Bis zum zweiten Vorlesen des Textes stehen fünf Minuten Zeit zur Verfügung, um Notizen anzufertigen.
5. Auch beim zweiten Vorlesen des Textes dürfen keine Notizen gemacht werden.
6. Nach dem zweiten Vorlesen beginnt die eigentliche Ausarbeitung der Antworten und des *comment*.

!

7. Die Verwendung eines Wörterbuchs ist nicht gestattet.
8. Der gesamte Teil A muss mindestens 150 Wörter umfassen.

Welche Inhalte werden behandelt?

Thema der 10. Klasse sind die USA, darum geht es in den meisten Texten um **amerikanische Landeskunde**. Es können aber auch allgemeine Bereiche wie **Schule, Ausbildung** und **Beruf** drankommen. In den bisherigen Arbeiten sind folgende Themen gewählt worden:

- **Politik**: Washington D.C.; President; Congress; political parties; Wahlkampf
- **Rassenbeziehungen**: Minderheiten, Indianer, Afroamerikaner, Asiaten
- **Landschaften und Lebensräume**: Midwest, Great Lakes, Wirtschaft, Verkehr, Kultur, Bevölkerung
- **Geschichte**: New England States, Boston, Harvard, The Boston Tea Party, Unabhängigkeit 1776, Civil Rights Movement
- **Geschichtliche Persönlichkeiten**: Franklin, Washington, Jefferson
- **Schulsystem**

Zu den Texten und Fragen:

Bei den Texten handelt es sich um allgemein verständliche, gut gegliederte Sachtexte oder erzählende Texte ohne viele Dialoge. Ein Spezialwissen ist für das Verständnis der Texte nicht erforderlich.

Die **Länge der Texte** beläuft sich auf etwa 370 bis 420 Wörter.

Meist werden **drei**, selten **vier Fragen** zu dem Text gestellt. Diese Fragen beziehen sich auf wesentliche Aussagen des Textes. Hinzu kommt eine Frage, die zu einer persönlichen Stellungnahme auffordert *(comment)*.

Die **Bewertung** jeder einzelnen Aufgabe (Inhaltspunkte) ist auf dem Aufgabenblatt am Rand vermerkt.

Durchführung Teil B – Übersetzung

1. Wortangaben werden an die Tafel geschrieben (ein- oder zweisprachig)
2. Übersetzung des Textes
3. Wörterbuch ist nicht gestattet

Es kommt in der Regel ein **allgemeiner** oder **amerikakundlicher Text** zum Lehrplan Klasse 10. Dabei handelt es sich um einen leicht verständlichen Sachtext, in dem gewöhnlich ein Satz eine schwierigere Konstruktion enthält.

Die **Textlänge** beträgt ca. 120 bis 130 Wörter.

Bewertung der ZKA

Die erweiterte Hörverstehensaufgabe (Teil A) wird nach **Sprachform und Inhalt** bewertet.

Die Note für die Sprachform ergibt sich aus dem Verhältnis von Wort- und Fehlerzahl.
Beispiel: 250 Wörter – 10 Fehler ergibt Note 3.

Bei einer sprachlich anspruchsvollen Ausdrucksweise kann der Fachlehrer die Note um eine halbe Note anheben. Eine stilistisch besonders dürftige Ausdrucksweise kann zu einem Notenabzug von einer halben Note führen. Bei Unterschreitung der Mindestwortzahl von 150 Wörtern erfolgt ein angemessener Notenabzug.

Die Note für **Inhalt** richtet sich nach den Inhaltspunkten, die der Schüler von der maximal zu vergebenden Punktzahl 12 erhält.
Beispiel: 10 Inhaltspunkte ergibt Note 2.

Starke deutsche Rechtschreibmängel können zu einem Notenabzug führen.

Die Übersetzung (Teil B) wird nach einer Fehlertabelle bewertet.
Beispiel: 10 Fehler ergibt Note 5.

Berechnung der Endnote von Teil A und Teil B:

	Gewichtung	Beispiel
Sprachform	x 4	3 x 4 = 12
Inhalt	x 3	2 x 3 = 6
Herübersetzung	x 3	5 x 3 = 15
		33 : 10 = 3,3 ≙ Endnote 3–

Nützliche Tipps

Die hier zusammengetragenen Tipps stammen zum größten Teil von Schülerinnen und Schülern, die diese Arbeit bereits geschrieben haben.

Erweiterte Hörverstehensaufgabe (Teil A)

Erstes Vorlesen

a) die an der Tafel stehenden **Wortangaben als roten Faden** beim Vorlesen verwenden und sich den Zusammenhang merken,

b) dem Lehrer während des Vorlesens genau auf den Mund schauen, um sprachliche Unterschiede herauszuhören,

c) den **Kontext** zu erfassen versuchen,

d) Beachtung von **Schlüsselwörtern**,

e) darauf achten, wann **Sprechpausen** gemacht werden (Ende eines Absatzes) oder die Stimme bestimmte Inhalte stärker betont (Hinweis auf wichtige Textaussage für die Beantwortung der Fragen)

Notizen

a) Fragen genau durchlesen,

b) zu jeder Frage der Reihenfolge nach Stichwörter notieren

Zweites Vorlesen

a) beim Vorlesen den Text mit den vorliegenden Fragen vergleichen und unterscheiden, welche Textpassagen sich auf Fragen beziehen und welche nicht,

b) besonders auf Fragen achten, zu denen noch keine Notizen nach dem ersten Vorlesen gemacht werden konnten

Nach dem zweiten Vorlesen

a) Ergänzung und gegebenenfalls Korrektur der ersten Aufzeichnungen,

b) Ausformulierung der Notizen – die angegebene Inhaltspunktzahl ist ein ungefährer Anhaltspunkt für die erwartete Länge der Antwort

Die **Mindestwortzahl** von 150 Wörtern muss bei weitem überschritten werden, um eine gute Inhaltsnote zu erreichen (so sind 250 bis 300 Wörter keine Seltenheit).

Hinweis

Die Punkte für die englische Sprachform sind im Allgemeinen schwieriger zu erreichen. Deshalb gilt: mit Bedacht formulieren, allzu hohes Risiko vermeiden, eher einfache Sätze bilden, genau auf Wortwahl und Grammatik achten (Einhaltung der Zeitenfolge, Verbformen, indirekte Rede); vor allem muss genug Zeit für genaues Durchlesen bleiben.
Bei dem *comment* kann man dem üblichen Dreierschema der Erörterung **Einleitung – Hauptteil – Schluss (persönliche Stellungnahme)** gewöhnlich folgen und so einen abgerundeten Eindruck erreichen. Es lohnt sich, eine Reihe von Ausdrücken parat zu haben, die man in jedem *comment* anwenden kann (→ S. 107).

Übersetzung (Teil B)

1. den gesamten Text durchlesen (es ergeben sich manchmal **Sinnergänzungen** im nachfolgenden Text),

2. **Rohübersetzung** erstellen: Sätze einzeln in Angriff nehmen; **Varianten** bei der Wortwahl notieren; sich für die beste entscheiden (unterstreichen);
bei **Schwierigkeiten** zunächst eine Lücke lassen (oder mit Bleistift schreiben und später darauf zurückkommen),

3. bei komplizierten Schachtelsätzen **Sinnstriche** in den Text einzeichnen, um die Satzkonstruktion besser zu erschließen,

4. Da in Klasse 10 von Ihnen noch kein absolut sicheres Stilgefühl erwartet wird, sollten Sie im Zweifelsfall eine wörtlichere Übersetzung einer allzu freien vorziehen. Zu freie Formulierungen vermitteln manchmal den Eindruck, dass eine Konstruktion nicht richtig erkannt worden ist.

5. Fremdwörter sollten vermieden werden, wenn es gleich gute oder geläufigere deutsche Entsprechungen gibt. Allerdings ist zu beachten, dass es Fälle gibt, bei denen das Fremdwort treffender ist. So ist z. B. *to accept* häufig nicht mit *annehmen*, sondern mit *akzeptieren* zu übersetzen. Auch muss zuweilen ein anderes Fremdwort zu Hilfe genommen werden, z. B. *level* – Niveau.

6. Folgende **sprachlichen Unterschiede** sind vor allem zu beachten:

a) Übersetzung englischer **Konstruktionen:** Auflösung der ing-Formen *present participle* und *gerund* und des *past participle* gewöhnlich durch Nebensätze (beim *past participle* erkennen, dass ein Relativpronomen ausgelassen wurde).

b) Unterschiedliche **Wortstellung:** im Englischen S-U-O-Regel/im Deutschen Nachstellung des Subjekts:

Beispiel: *I thought so* – Das dachte ich mir/*The Declaration of Independence was to prove more significant* – Bedeutsamer sollte die Unabhängigkeitserklärung werden.
Oder: Im deutschen Nebensatz steht das Prädikat am Satzende:
Beispiel: *When the immigrants arrived in America* – Als die Einwanderer in Amerika ankamen

c) Englisches **Passiv** entspricht normalerweise deutscher Übersetzung mit *man:*
Beispiel: *They were promised higher wages* – Man versprach ihnen höhere Löhne.

d) Englisches **Verb** entspricht manchmal deutschem **Adverb**:
to happen to do sth – etw zufällig tun

e) Vorsicht vor **Wortfallen:**
Beispiel: *self-conscious* – schüchtern, verlegen; nicht: selbstbewusst

7. Zur Vorbereitung der Übersetzung empfiehlt es sich, die Liste wichtiger Wörter zum landeskundlichen Amerikawortschatz (→ S. 114) gut zu lernen.
Da die ZKA sich ausschließlich auf den Lehrplan Klasse 10 bezieht, sind Wiederholungen im Ausdruck unvermeidbar.

Zur Arbeit mit diesem Buch

Das Buch ist so aufgebaut, dass zunächst die komplette Prüfungsaufgabe mit allen Fragen und den erlaubten Hilfen vorgegeben wird. Aus rechtlichen Gründen haben wir nicht die Originalprüfungstexte abgedruckt, sondern sie in einer modifizierten Form wiedergegeben. Die Inhalte und der Schwierigkeitsgrad entsprechen aber den Anforderungen dieser Prüfung. Im Lösungsteil wird dann der mögliche Weg zu einem guten Ergebnis exemplarisch aufgezeigt.

Im ersten Schritt werden die **Notizen** aufgelistet, die Sie sich nach dem Vorlesen des Textes machen dürfen. Sie sind bewusst umfangreich gehalten, um die ganze Bandbreite hilfreicher Stichwörter zu erfassen.

Im nächsten Schritt werden die Notizen zu einem **Text** zusammengeschrieben. Die **linke Spalte** gibt die Musterlösung an. In der **rechten Spalte** erscheinen alternative Formulierungen, Worterklärungen und Hinweise auf grammatische Formen, die zu beachten sind, weil sie häufig zu Fehlern führen.

Als zusätzliche Hilfe werden **Wortfelder** und **Themen der Grammatik,** die einen engen Bezug zu dem Prüfungstext haben, gesondert behandelt.

Als Ergänzung zur **Übersetzung** erscheinen **Anmerkungen**, die auf problematische Stellen im Text verweisen und Übersetzungsvarianten vorstellen.

Die gewählten Hilfen und Tipps lassen sich auch auf andere Texte und Aufgabenstellungen übertragen. Es lohnt sich daher, sie genauer zu betrachten.

Folgende Abkürzungen werden verwendet:

adj	adjective	n	noun
adv	adverb	pl	Plural
AE	American English	R	Rechtschreibung
BE	British English	sg	Singular
D	Deutsche Entsprechung	vb	verb
G	Grammatik	W	Wort/Wortschatz

Korrekturzeichen S. 15 – 26

I)	Inhalt	W)	Wiederholung
Sp)	Sprache	Z)	Zeichensetzung
St)	Stil	V)	Lücke

Die Vorbereitung auf die Klassenarbeit

Sie können die Realsituation durchspielen, indem Sie sich den Text von Freunden oder Eltern vorlesen lassen. Wie in der Prüfungssituation bearbeiten Sie dann die Aufgaben in 90 Minuten und vergleichen Ihr Ergebnis mit dem Lösungsvorschlag des Autors. Beim *comment* ist ein solches Abgleichen natürlich nicht möglich, Sie können aber überprüfen, ob Sie Redewendungen richtig benutzt haben und ob in der Rechtschreibung alles glatt gelaufen ist.

Sie können das Buch auch dazu verwenden, um mögliche Lösungswege zu einer guten Note nachzuvollziehen. Darüber hinaus bieten die Hinweise auf alternative Formulierungen die Möglichkeit den eigenen Wortschatz zu erweitern.

Da die Themen der Zentralen Klassenarbeit meist der amerikanischen Landeskunde entnommen sind, tauchen bestimmte Vokabeln immer wieder auf. Sie sind auf den Seiten 114 – 119 zusammengetragen.

Redewendungen, die für den *comment* immer wieder verwendet werden, finden Sie auf den Seiten 107 – 113. Wenn Sie sich diese Dinge gut einprägen, werden Sie bei den meisten Aufgabenstellungen davon profitieren können.

Für die Hilfe bei der Erstellung des Manuskripts sei an dieser Stelle
Jim Holme aus Newton Abbot, Devon,
Catherine Weston, University of Hull, und
Corinna Spann vom Int. Dolmetscherinstitut Stuttgart
herzlich gedankt.

Klassenarbeit 1 (Beispielarbeiten)

Teil A Erweiterte Hörverstehensaufgabe

Wortangaben zu Teil A

achievement .... hier: Leistung
extracurricular .... außerhalb des Lehrplans

Text

Americans have always considered public education to be the ladder to success in life. Statistics reveal that this opinion has become more and more widespread during the last 100 years: in 1900, for example, only about 10 % of young Americans went to college. Today more than 30 % of adult Americans have been to college, and there are some 3,000 different colleges and universities to choose from. The rapid growth of public universities financed by government money has made this development possible. Today a lot of parents who couldn't go to college in their youth are delighted to see their children attend.

Although Americans know that a good education leads to success, they do not think that intellectual achievement, which is the main purpose of going to school, is the only significant element for success in life. A competitive personality and a strong will are regarded as equally important. The development of social and political skills is also considered to be of great importance.

To encourage Americans to develop these skills, schools have included several extracurricular activities in their daily life. Sports, especially competitive sports such as football, basketball, and baseball, are treated very seriously in teaching students the "winning spirit". Sometimes, sports may even become more important to some families than the academic programs carried out in the classrooms.

Student government is also designed to develop competitive, political and social skills. Elections are held, in which candidates have the opportunity to compete for the votes of their fellow students to become student government officers. These officers have little real influence over the central decisions of the school; nevertheless, the process of running for office is regarded as good training in developing competitive skills. Accepting responsibility for a number of minor matters if elected can be seen as a useful step towards leadership in adult life.

Sports and student government are not the only ways in which American schools widen the experience of their students. There are many clubs and activities, all aimed at helping the student to become a responsible citizen. Many parents watch their children's extracurricular progress with as much interest and concern as they do their intellectual achievement in the classroom. (364 words)

Fragen zum Text

1 Answer the following questions in complete sentences. Keep to the information given in the text.

a) How has the attitude of Americans to public education changed over the last 100 years. **(2 Punkte)**

b) What qualities do Americans believe their children need for success? **(2 Punkte)**

c) How do American schools prepare their students for a successful life? **(4 Punkte)**

2 Today students in secondary schools have to spend a period of time in offices, factories etc. What is your opinion of this kind of work experience? **(4 Punkte)**

Teil B Übersetzung

Wortangaben zu Teil B

to reject .... ablehnen
issue .... hier: Frage, Problem

Text

Computers play an essential part in American society today, but their place in schools is not yet determined. Some schools are still rejecting the computer revolution, while many others are seeking to deal with it in a way that supports the educational progress of their students.

The demands of education, however, cannot be met by relying on computers alone. The answer lies instead in studying the issues and discussing various points of view in order to reach a conclusion. As computers continue to play a dominant role in daily life, we must make sure that everyone will be able to understand and use them. This is the best way to use the new technology, to help people learn, communicate and work together. (121 words)

1 Beispiel für eine sehr gute Schülerarbeit

Teil A Erweiterte Hörverstehensaufgabe

1 Notizen

a) – public education always been considered to be ladder to success
- attitude has become more widespread in the last 100 years
- more pupils go to college: 1900 10 % – now: 30 %
- more colleges I
- state gives money
- more extracurricular activities I

b) – intellectual achievement
- strong will, competitive personality
- social and political skills

c) American schools train these qualities by including extra-curricular activities:
- sports: competitive sports (baseball, football, basketball) spirit of winning Sp
- student government: school officers, accept responsibility for minor manners, useful step towards leadership Sp
- lots of clubs and other activities at school: often regarded by parents with as much interest as academic subjects

Kommentar

Viele Schüler notieren zu viele Einzelheiten bei den ersten Fragen und vernachlässigen dann die folgenden. Im Gegensatz dazu hat Schülerin A darauf geachtet, dass die meisten Punkte bei Frage c) vergeben werden. Die Anmerkungen sind ausgewogen und durchdacht. Andererseits wird deutlich, dass kleinere inhaltliche wie auch vereinzelte sprachliche Mängel der Ausführung (z. B. der Hörfehler *manners* statt *matters*) bereits in den Notizen vorhanden sind.

2 *Comment* – Notizen

Einleitung

- American students spend time in factories, offices etc.
- in Germany work experience becomes more important, too
- reasons?

Hauptteil

- work experience important to get to know the "real world" experience prepares them for time after graduation
- helps the young people to find a suitable job otherwise wrong job,might cause problems Sp
- learn to work in teams and on their own, must take responsibilty, less problems in finding a job Sp

Schluss

- work experience very positive for students introduced into more and more countries

Kommentar

Eine gut strukturierte Gliederung in Form des traditionellen Dreierschemas einer Erörterung. Die Einleitung führt in Form einer Frage auf den Hauptteil hin, der drei wichtige Gründe zugunsten der *work experiences* behandelt. Die abschließende verallgemeinernde Äußerung ergibt sich folgerichtig aus dem Hauptteil.

Ausführung

1

a) Public education has always been considered to be the ladder to success by Americans. This attitude has become even more widespread in the last 100 years and as a result much more pupils go to college. V 1900 10 % 1, 1, 1
of young people had a college degree, now 30% have one. Of course I
there are more colleges nowadays. The state has given and still gives money to them to make this possible. [Besides this,there are more and I [ ]
more extracurricular activities.] 1,5 P

b) The qualities they regard as most significant for success are intellectual achievement, a strong will and a competitive personality. These three qualities are supposed to be equal. But social and political skills are said to be important for success, too.

2 P

c) American schools encourage these qualities to give their (pupils) the s.o.
opportunity to succeed in life by offering extra-curricular activities. Two
of them are student government and sports, especially competitive
sports like baseball, football and basketball. They aim to give the spirit of 1, ½
winning. Student government is said to be a positive experience because
the elected "school officers" accept responsibility for minor manners 1
which is a good training for leadership. Moreover there are lots of clubs
and other activities at school, which are often regarded by parents with
as much interest as the academic subjects.

4 P

2

Today, American students in secondary school must spend some time in factories, offices etc. In Germany, this kind of work experience is becoming more and more important,too. But why is this kind of experience said to be so important? Let's have a look at the reasons.

First of all work experience is important for students to get to know the
"real world". It's easier for them to manage their situation after their
graduation if they've once before been faced with the working life of 1
an average adult. The experience prepares them for the time after their
graduation.

Moreover it helps the young people to find a suitable job where they ½
can use their skills and which they like. Otherwise they might get a job
but soon realize that it's not the right one for them, which might cause
problems.

Furthermore (pupils) learn to work in teams and on their own which is s.o.
very important today. V This way they learn to work together with other St
people but also to take responsibility. Pupils who learn this will have less Z, ½
problems in finding a job and integrating into their new team at work.

I'm sure that we can draw the conclusion that this kind of work experience is a very positive experience for students. I think it will be introduced into more and more countries because of the strong reasons I've mentioned. (439 W)

4 P

Insgesamt:	**Sprache**	7,5 P
	Inhalt	11,5 P

Bewertung Teil A

Inhalt

In 1 a) (Z. 4) fehlt die Information *3,000 colleges*, außerdem wurde in Z. 6/7 eine zwar nicht falsche, aber hier überflüssige Tatsache angeführt, die für Frage 1 c) bestimmt ist; deshalb nicht die volle Punktzahl, sondern Punktabzug von 0,5 P. > 1,5 P.
1 b) und 1 c) sind vollständig beantwortet, sodass hier die maximale Punktzahl vergeben werden konnte.
Der *Comment* in 2 ist derart gut durchstrukturiert und inhaltlich gelungen, dass die Gesamtpunktzahl von 4 P. in Anbetracht der vorgegebenen Zeit von 90 Minuten mehr als gerechtfertigt erscheint.

Sprache

Schülerin A verfügt bereits über ein beachtliches sprachliches Niveau, sodass nur wenige Mängel zu berichtigen waren:

Zeile

3 *many more students*: Wegen des nachfolgenden Substantivs im Plural muss es *many* heißen, auch wenn man im Deutschen „viel mehr" sagt; im Text ist von *college* die Rede, deshalb muss es *students*, nicht *pupils* heißen.

3 *In 1900*: Jahresangabe mit Präposition

15 *They shall create the winning spirit*: falsche bzw. ungeschickte Formulierung

17 *for minor matters*: falsches Wort

27 *they've ever/already been faced with*: *(ever/already mit present perfect)*

30 *it helps young people:* (Gattungsnamen ohne Artikel, → S. 33)

35 *In this way* ist korrekteres Englisch

36 *fewer problems* ist korrekt, auch wenn umgangssprachlich manchmal *less* mit Nomen im Plural zu hören ist.

Übersetzung Teil B

Computer spielen heute eine wesentliche Rolle in der amerikanischen Gesellschaft, aber ihr Platz in den Schulen ist noch nicht bestimmt. Einige Schulen lehnen die Computerrevolution immer noch ab, während viele andere versuchen, mit ihr in einer Weise umzugehen, die die edukationellen Fortschritte ihrer Schüler fördert. 1

Die Bildungsanforderungen können jedoch nicht dadurch erfüllt werden, dass man sich allein auf Computer verlässt. Die Antwort besteht stattdessen darin, die Probleme zu untersuchen und über verschiedenartige Meinungen zu diskutieren, um eine Schlussfolgerung zu ziehen. Da Computer weiterhin eine beherrschende Rolle im täglichen Leben spielen, müssen wir sicherstellen, dass jeder dazu fähig sein wird, sie zu verstehen und sie zu benutzen. Dies ist die beste Art und Weise, wie man die neue Technologie anwenden kann, um den Menschen dabei zu helfen, zu lernen, zu kommunizieren und zusammenzuarbeiten.

1 F

Bewertung Teil B

Bei dieser wortgetreuen und gleichzeitig gewandten Übersetzung sind nur wenige Anmerkungen bzw. Varianten hinzuzufügen:

Zeile

2 *determined:* festgelegt/klar umrissen

3 *to deal with:* fertig zu werden mit/sie zu handhaben

4 *educational progress:* die pädagogischen Fortschritte/Fortschritte in der Ausbildung

7 *to reach a conclusion:* zu einem Schluss kommen

9/10 *to help people learn ...;* beim Lernen, bei der Kommunikation und der Zusammenarbeit zu helfen

(Zeilenangaben beziehen sich auf den Text auf Seite 14.)

Berechnungsbogen

Teil A					
Punkte	11,5				
Inhaltsnote	1	x	3	=	3
Wortzahl	439				
Fehlerzahl	7,5				
Note/Inhaltsnote	1,5	x	4	=	6
Teil B					
Fehler	1				
Note	1	x	3	=	3
Summe					12:10
Endnote					= **1,25**

Lösungen

2 Beispiel für eine schlechte Schülerarbeit

Teil A Erweiterte Hörverstehensaufgabe

1 Notizen

a) – at the beginnig only 10 % have been to college	Sp, I
– now many children are going to college	I
– many parents did not have an aducation so they want their children to have it	I[ ], Sp
– the stat has seen that the people have more success when they had been to college	Sp Sp
b) – They think academic programms are very important and college is very important	Sp
– college is a leather to succes	Sp
c) – There are extracurricular things for children like sports and other activities (basketball, football and baseball) But academic programms are important, too	s.o.I[ ]
– There are clubs	

Kommentar

Die Gliederung enthält eine Vielzahl sprachlicher und inhaltlicher Mängel, die eine stark fehlerhafte Ausführung erwarten lassen. Einige der sprachlichen Fehler *(beginnig, aducation, stat)* sind wohl nur durch den Zeitdruck zu erklären, unter dem die Notizen aufgeschrieben worden sind. Andere, vor allem Zeitfehler, werden unkorrigiert in die Ausführung übernommen. Inhaltlich sind Ungenauigkeiten (z. B. Zahlen in 1a), unwichtige Argumente (1 a, 1 c) und Auslassungen (in 1 c fehlen 50 % des Inhalts, nämlich *student government*) zu beanstanden. Auch wenn Schülerin B sich bei der Ausführung noch an einige Dinge genauer erinnern wird, die nicht in der Gliederung erwähnt wurden, so ist doch bereits abzusehen, dass sie von den möglichen acht Inhaltspunkten vielleicht nur noch die Hälfte wird erzielen können.

2 *Comment* – Notizen

Eine Gliederung ist nicht vorgenommen worden.

Ausführung

a) At the beginning of 1900 only 10% of the people had been to	1
college. Many people didn't have the chance or the money to go to	I
college or to attend school. But those who had been to college had	
more chances for a successfull life. So the state began to built a lot	$\frac{1}{2}$, 1
of new colleges and universities for the people, because they knew,	
that they will have better chances to be successfull in later times.	Z, 1, s.o., 1
At the moment many people go to college or attend school. The	1, s.o., $\frac{1}{2}$, Z
statistics show that over 40 % of the people had been to college	1, I
and have a successfull life.	s.o.
	VI
	1 P
b) They think, that college is a leather to success. It is very important to	Z, 1
attend school and to go to college. There are academic programms	$\frac{1}{2}$
which are very important for the people in their later life. And they	$\frac{1}{2}$
think, that extracurricular programms are very important, too.	Z, s.o
The children had to have good results in school or in college. They	$\frac{1}{2}$, 1
say, that they have to have the wish to be successfull, to win and	Z, s.o.
to have good results.	IW
	VI
	0,5 P
c) They train them to have very good marks. They had to have the	1, s.o.
wish to be successfull. And extracurricular programms are very	s.o.
important, too. They learn in extracurricular programms like	s.o.
football, baseball and basketball how the feeling is to win and to be	1
successfull. So they made clubs for sports and other activities. They	s.o., 1
saw, that a good achievement in school or in college is a leather	Z, s.o.
for V successfull life.	$\frac{1}{2}$, 1, s.o.
They won't have so much problems in later times or in their life.	1, s.o., s.o.
	I
	1,5 P

2

First of all I think it is a great idea, that students in secondary	Z
schools have to spend a period of time in offices or factories or so. I	St,
think that the students can learn there for their life. They learn how	$\frac{1}{2}$, s.o.
to work, to be together and communicate with other people. They	
learn there how to earn their own money and how it is like in their	1
later life when they are on their own. They get a lot of experience	s.o.
and they can see, that life isn't so easy like they thougt before. But	Z, 1, $\frac{1}{2}$
it is important, too, that they do not spend too much time for it,	Z, $\frac{1}{2}$, I
because they have to learn for school and to have other important	
activities. (394w)	
	2,5 P

Insgesamt:	Sprache	19,5 F
	Inhalt	6 P

Bewertung Teil A

1 Inhalt

Wie in der Gliederung schon ersichtlich, sind in allen Antworten Ungenauigkeiten, Auslassungen, Wiederholungen (W) oder Zusätze zu beanstanden.

a) In Zeile 2 findet sich eine eigene, zusätzliche Information, in der vorletzten Zeile steht statt 30 % nun 40 %, die Information *3,000 colleges* (VI) fehlt.

b) Es ist nur eine grobe inhaltliche Information gegeben; es fehlen zentrale Aussagen wie *competitive personality, strong will, social and political skills*, außerdem gehört der Hinweis auf *extracurricular activities* zu 1 c).

c) Hier fällt eine für den Inhalt missverständliche Verwendung von *they*, eine Wiederholung der Aussage und das Fehlen der Ausführungen zu *student government* auf.

Der *Comment* ist inhaltlich besser gelungen und etwas flüssiger geschrieben als die *Comprehension* Aufgabe. Insgesamt vermisst man die Strukturierung, das Dreier-Schema und deutliche Absätze zur Markierung der einzelnen Schritte. Das Fehlen einer Gliederung macht sich deutlich bemerkbar.

Sprache

Schülerin B verfügt über geringere Englischkenntnisse; grammatikalisch hat sie große Schwierigkeiten, ihr Wortschatz ist äußerst begrenzt (siehe die vielen Wiederholungsfehler).

1 a)

Zeile

1 *In 1900* oder *At the beginning/At the turn of the 20th century*

4 *successful* (-ful als Nachsilbe wird immer mit einem „l" geschrieben.)

4 *to build (built – built)*

6 *they knew that they would have:* indirekte Rede

6 *in the future:* die Formulierung im Text ist falsch

7 *are going or attending: present progressive* wegen *at the moment*

7 *Statistics* ohne Artikel

8/9 *show ... have been ... and have* – die Zeitstufe muss eingehalten werden (*present – present perfect*)

1 b)

10 *ladder*: Leiter zum Erfolg; Wortverwechslung

11 *programmes* (BE) oder *programs* (AE)

12 *in their later lives*: im E. ist man konsequenter und setzt das Substantiv „Leben" in den Plural, da es sich auf mehrere Personen bezieht: z. B. *They lost their lives.* – Sie verloren ihr Leben.

14 *Children:* nicht eingeschränkte Gattungsnamen stehen ohne den best. Artikel (s. S. 33)

14 *have to have:* die Erzählzeit ist nicht eingehalten worden (siehe vorheriger und nachfolgender Satz)

1 c)

17 *Schools* oder *Students*: unklarer Bezug durch *they*

20 *what it feels like/what it is like:* nicht *how*

21 *founded/introduced/established:* unpassendes Verb

23 *ladder to:* falsche Präposition

23 *a successful life:* fehlender Artikel

24 *many problems*

2

25 *students*: ohne Artikel, (s. 1b, Z. 14)

27 *what it is like*

29 *as easy as* (Vergleich)

29 *thought*

30 *spend on:* falsche Präposition

Teil B Übersetzung

Computer spielen eine unersetzliche Rolle im americanischen	$\frac{1}{2}$, R, $\frac{1}{2}$
Sozialleben heute, aber ihr Platz an den Schulen wurde bis jetzt	St, 1
noch nicht vereinbart. Einige Schulen lehnen die Computerrevolution	1
immer noch ab, während viele andere versuchen in einem Weg, der	1, St, 1,
den schulischen Fortschritt ihrer Studenten unterstützt, mit ihnen zu	St, 1,
handeln.	1
Die Forderungen von Schulabschlüssen, wie auch immer, können	1, 1
nicht nur mit dem Beruhen auf die Computer getroffen werden. Die	$\frac{1}{2}$, 1
Antworten lügen anstatt die Probleme zu studieren und verschiedene	$\frac{1}{2}$, 1
Sichtpunkte auszudisskutieren um damit eine V zu erreichen. Als die	1, R, Z,
Computer weiter machten eine dominante Rolle im alltäglichen Leben	1, 1
zu spielen, müssen wir klar machen, dass jeder in der Lage sein wird sie	$\frac{1}{2}$, 1
zu verstehen und sie zu gebrauchen. Das ist der beste (Weg), die neue	1, Z
Technologie zu gebrauchen, um den Leuten zu helfen, zu lernen, zu	s. o.
kommunizieren und miteinander zu arbeiten.	
	17,5 F

Lösungen

Bewertung Teil B (S. 14)

Aufgrund der vielen sprachlichen Fehler musste hier die Note „ungenügend" gegeben werden:

Zeile	
1	*essential:* die Übersetzung unersetzlich ist zu stark; richtig: wesentlich/grundlegend
1	*American:* deutscher Rechtschreibfehler
1	*society:* genauer: Gesellschaft
1	*today:* im D besser vorgestellt zu *play:* spielen heute
2	*is determined:* im D falsches Wort und falsche Zeitform (Präteritum) ist noch nicht festgelegt/klar umrissen
3	*to deal with:* fertig werden mit/umgehen mit
3	*with it:* mit ihnen: falscher Bezug; richtig: damit (mit ihr), auf *computer revolution* bezogen
3	*way:* hat zwei Bedeutungen a) Weg – b) Art/Weise; hier Weise; weiter unten Z. 9 würde auch Weg Sinn machen
3	*supports:* stilistisch besser: fördert
4	*students:* da es sich hier um Schulen handelt, ist nur Schüler möglich
4	*progress:* stilistisch besser im D: Fortschritte
5	*education:* Schulabschlüsse viel zu eng; richtig: Bildung/Erziehung,

also: Bildungsanforderungen/pädagogische/erzieherische Erfordernisse

5 *met:* kann hier nicht wörtlich übersetzt werden: idiomatischer Ausdruck: *to meet the demands:* die Anforderungen erfüllen

5 *however:* ganz schwerer Fehler; es muss natürlich jedoch heißen

5 *by relying on:* unschönes D; besser Nebensatz: dadurch dass/indem man sich auf... verlässt/dass man ... vertraut

6 *answer:* genauer Singular: Antwort

6 *lies:* Wortverwechslung; natürlich muss es heißen: die Antwort liegt darin

6 *instead:* hier nicht anstatt; dies ergibt einen völlig falschen Bezug im Verlauf des Satzes, deshalb Konstruktionsfehler; richtig: stattdessen

7 *points of view:* zu wörtliche Übersetzung; richtig: Standpunkte/Meinungen/Ansichten

6 *discussing:* R-Fehler

7 *conclusion:* Schluss(folgerung); *to reach a conclusion:* eine Schlussfolgerung ziehen

7 *as:* begründend: da

7 *continue to play:* zu wörtliche Übersetzung; richtig: weiterhin spielen

8 *dominant:* Wort ist einzudeutschen: beherrschend

8 *make sure:* richtig muss es heißen: uns überzeugen/uns vergewissern

Berechnungsbogen

Teil A					
Punkte	6				
Inhaltsnote	4	x	3	=	12
Wortzahl	394				
Fehlerzahl	19,5				
Note/Inhaltsnote	4+	x	4	=	15
Teil B					
Fehler	17,5				
Note	6	x	3	=	18
Summe					45:10
Endnote					= **4,5**

Klassenarbeit 2

Teil A Erweiterte Hörverstehensaufgabe

Wortangaben zu Teil A

Harry Han .... proper name
Seoul .... capital of South Korea
Hyan Ho Han .... proper name
pharmacist .... chemist
to enrol .... to register as a student at a university
attendant .... s.o. whose job is to serve people in a place such as a gas station
charity .... Wohltätigkeit

Text

Harry Han is just one of many well-educated Asians who have recently decided to begin new lives in Los Angeles.

When his flight from *Seoul* landed in Los Angeles in 1975, Han's name was *Hyan Ho Han*. He was an experienced *pharmacist* who had qualified at a Korean University. He brought his wife, two children and about $4,000 with him.

Han, 41, had been granted a visa in Seoul, thanks to a U.S. law that encourages immigrants who have job skills needed in America. At that time, pharmacists were welcomed with open arms.

Han *enrolled* straight away at a local two-year college to gain the necessary extra qualifications to open a pharmacy in California. When he wasn't in the classroom he worked as much as possible, sometimes 12 to 16 hours a day, as a gas station *attendant* for $2 an hour.

Like many immigrants, Han realised that he needed to work hard in order to survive in his new country, but also that hard work paid off.

Han was a very good worker, and after only two years in America his employer gave him a job managing a downtown gas station that was doing badly. Soon Han's station was selling four times as much gas as it had before. At this time, Han was saving $60 of every $100 he earned. Within three years he had enough money to buy a house.

He was so successful in money matters that he was forced to change his plans for the future, which seemed to be in selling gas rather than pills.

"I wanted to finish school, but things were very hard ... I was so tired ...," Han said with a smile, and explained why he abandoned his plans to make a career as a pharmacist.

Like other immigrants, Han started to buy gas stations, which were quite cheap at the time. American business people did not want to own them because of the worldwide oil crisis.

"We Korean people use our brains," Han said proudly. "We are clever and very friendly!" Now Han has become a U.S. citizen and owns five gas stations that earn him between $10,000 and $15,000 per month. Recently he bought his third house, and his children are doing well in public schools. He is active in a number of local charity organizations. His aim is to buy one more gas station every year. (402 words)

Fragen zum Text

1 Answer the following questions in complete sentences. Keep to the information given in the text.

a) What was Mr Han's situation when he came to Los Angeles? **(2 Punkte)**

b) How did he succeed in his chosen business career? **(3 Punkte)**

c) Describe the Han family's life style today. **(3 Punkte)**

2 State your opinion on the following question.

Discuss the advantages and disadvantages of accepting only educated immigrants into a country. **(4 Punkte)**

Teil B Übersetzung

Wortangaben zu Teil B

unbearable .... unerträglich

Text

To all immigrants – to those who had suffered for their religious beliefs, to those who had refused to serve in the armed forces, to those who dreamed of greater democracy, to those who had lived in *unbearable* poverty, America was the Promised Land. All had a vision of a better life, and most of them did create such a life for themselves and for their children. The earliest immigrants had settled all over the North and West, and had become farmers and industrial workers in about equal numbers. But because it took money to start a farm, because the best land was gone, because there were jobs in the cities, the new arrivals moved to the industrial areas in the East and Middle West.

(122 words)

Teil A Erweiterte Hörverstehensaufgabe

1 Notizen

a)
- experienced pharmacist (had qualified at a Korean university)
- wife, two children, $4,000
- had been granted a visa (job skills needed in the USA)

b)
- enrolled at a local two-year college (extra qualifications to open a pharmacy in California)
- worked as a gas station attendant for $2 an hour
- hard work paid off
- was given a job managing a downtown gas station
- abandoned plans to make a career as a pharmacist
- started to buy gas stations

c)
- US citizen
- owns five gas stations
- earns him between $10,000 and 15,000
- bought third house
- children do well at public schools
- active in local charity organizations

Ausführung

a) **When Mr Han came to Los Angeles,** he was **an experienced** pharmacist **who had qualified at** a Korean university. He brought his wife, two children and about **$4,000** with him. Han had been granted a visa, because his job skills were **needed** in the USA.

W On his arrival in LA, Mr Han
W a successful
W with a degree from
G $ Zeichen vor Zahl
W wanted

b) Han enrolled at a local **two-year** college to **gain** the extra qualifications __ to open a pharmacy in California. Moreover he started to work as a gas station attendant for **$2 an hour** and soon realized that hard work **paid off**. After two years

G two-year – kein Plural -s
W get
W needed
W a very low hourly wage
W would lead to success

he was given **a job managing** a downtown gas station. Han was so successful **in this business** that he **abandoned** his plans to make **a** career as **a pharmacist** and started to buy gas stations.	W the job of manager of W in money matters W gave up G to make a career G Berufsbezeichnung mit Artikel
c) Today Han is a US citizen. He **owns** five gas stations **that earn him** between $10,000 and $15,000 per month. **Recently** he bought his third house. His children **are doing** well in public schools and he is **active in a number of** charity organizations.	W is the owner of W from which he earns W Not long ago G present progressive W involved with W several

2 *Comment* – Notizen

Einleitung

In the text above the Korean pharmacist was accepted into the USA because of his job skills. Today in western countries similar proposals to restrict immigration.

Hauptteil

advantages:

- restriction of unwanted immigrants
- educated immigrants constitute a badly needed workforce
- they are welcomed by the native population
- the natives profit from their skills
- they are not among the unemployed

disadvantages:

- richer countries have a moral obligation to help the poor and the oppressed
- US basically a country of immigrants, most of them did not have the necessary skills when they immigrated
- colleges and have become famous specialists and scientists

Schluss

personal opinion: quite understandable to offer "green cards" to a limited number of highly qualified specialists, but this should not mean a general restriction or even a complete rejection of uneducated immigrants

Ausführung

The text above **gives us** the **example** of a Korean pharmacist who, under an immigration **law**, was **admitted to** the United States because of his special **skills**. In the same way at present western European countries are trying to **come to terms with** rising immigration by **willing** to accept only educated people. What are the pros and cons of such plans?

W discussed, case
W act; W allowed to enter
W qualifications
W to deal with/manage
W being prepared

On the one hand such a **regulation** offers a number of advantages. It means a **restriction** of **unwanted** immigrants. Moreover educated people constitute **a badly** needed industrial workforce that may help to **strengthen the economy**. Additionally they are welcome as the native population **profits** from their job skills and as there is no **danger** that they will become unemployed and need to be supported by social welfare.

W decision
W limitation; W unemployable
W an urgently
W promote; G *economy* immer mit best. Artikel
W benefits
W risk

But this is just one **aspect of the issue**. To my mind in the **world of today** the richer countries have a moral **obligation** to share their **wealth** and to offer help to the **poor** and the oppressed. Furthermore the history of the USA, a **typical country of** immigrants, **shows how** the nation has been **shaped** and built up by people who mostly did not have **the necessary** skills when they immigrated. Even today we see that many unqualified immigrants from **overseas**, mainly from Asia, are among the **best** students of US colleges and have become **famous** specialists and scientists.

W side of the coin, argument
W modern world
W duty
W prosperity
W needy (Bedürftigen)
W country largely populated by
W proves that; W formed
W useful
W abroad
W ablest/most talented
W well-known

In conclusion, I would like to **state** that it is quite **understandable** that a country offers "green cards" to **a limited number** of highly qualified specialists. But this should not **mean** a general restriction or even a complete **rejection of** uneducated immigrants.

W suggest
W comprehensible

W relatively few
W imply/signify

W ban on

GRAMMATIK: Der Gebrauch des bestimmten Artikels

Der bestimmte Artikel wird nicht verwendet vor folgenden Substantivgruppen, wenn diese allgemein verwendet werden:
- Gattungsnamen (*students, children, boys, youth*)
- Stoffnamen (*coal, oil, gold, water)*
- abstrakte Begriffe (*nature, self-determination, destruction, life, freedom*)
- kollektive Begriffe (*man, society, mankind*)
- Ausnahmen: z. B. *the government, the economy*

Der bestimmte Artikel wird verwendet, wenn diese Substantivgruppen näher bestimmt sind, a) durch einen of-Genitiv, b) durch einen Nebensatz:
- *the youth of today, the children of our class*
- *the coal that is found in the Appalachians*
- *the life they lead, the freedom to be Indians*
- *the society they live in*

Bei vorausgehendem Adjektiv ist zu beachten, dass der Artikel nicht steht, wenn Adjektiv und Substantiv eine Einheit bilden:
technological progress, American life, human nature, public opinion, European history, economic growth, private property, modern technology, British literature, German industry

Beachte:
most in der Bedeutung „die meisten" in Verbindung mit einem Substantiv wird immer ohne Artikel verwendet: *most people think, most houses in our town.*

Teil B Übersetzung

Für alle Einwanderer – für diejenigen, die wegen ihrer religiösen Überzeugungen gelitten hatten, für die, die sich geweigert hatten, in der Armee zu dienen, für die, die von mehr Demokratie träumten, für die, die in unerträglicher Armut gelebt hatten, war Amerika das gelobte Land. Alle hatten die Vorstellung eines besseren Lebens und die meisten von ihnen schufen sich in der Tat solch ein Leben für sich und ihre Kinder. Die ersten Einwanderer hatten sich überall im Norden und Westen angesiedelt und waren zahlenmäßig in etwa gleich Farmer und Industriearbeiter geworden. Aber weil es Geld kostete, eine Farm aufzubauen, weil das beste Land vergeben war, weil es Arbeitsplätze in den Städten gab, zogen die Neuankömmlinge in die Industriegebiete im Osten und Mittleren Westen.

Anmerkungen

Zeile	
1	*for:* aufgrund
1	*their religious beliefs:* ihrer religiösen Einstellung, ihres Glaubens
2	*refused:* es abgelehnt hatten/die den Militärdienst verweigert hatten
4	*Promised Land:* das verheißene/gepriesene Land
4	*vision:* Vision, Traum, Wunschbild
4	*did create:* bejahtes *to do* in verstärkender Funktion: tatsächlich, wirklich; z. B. *They did play well:* Sie spielten wirklich gut – Beachte auch: *Do come in* – Kommen Sie doch herein; *You do look tired.* – Sie sehen aber müde aus.
5	*such a:* ein derartiges
6	*settled:* niedergelassen
7	*in about equal numbers:* etwa gleichmäßig verteilt
7	*because it took money:* weil man Geld benötigte/brauchte
7	*farmer/farm:* da es sich um landestypische Ausdrücke handelt, ist es besser, diese hier stehen zu lassen
7	*to start:* gründen
8	*was gone:* verteilt war
8	*jobs:* Arbeit; unbedingt das unschöne „Jobs" im Deutschen vermeiden
9	*arrivals:* hier nicht in der Bedeutung „Ankunft", sondern personifiziert „Ankömmlinge"

Klassenarbeit 3

Teil A Erweiterte Hörverstehensaufgabe

Wortangaben zu Teil A

Supreme Court	Oberster Gerichtshof
Arkansas	state in the South of the USA
Central High	a high school in Little Rock
Little Rock	capital of Arkansas
Eisenhower	President of the USA (1953–1961)
to enrol	to register as a student at a school
anniversary	Jahrestag
remedial classes	classes for students who are slower at learning
segregation	Rassentrennung

Text

In 1954 the US *Supreme Court* ordered all public schools to admit black students. By 1957 a few schools in the state of *Arkansas* were still refusing to integrate; *Central High* in *Little Rock*, for example, had no black pupils. However, a group of nine black teenagers decided that had to change. All over the world people watched their struggle against racism in this southern town. This was one of the highlights of the civil rights movement, that was determined to end segregation in the US.

On September 4, 1957, the black teenagers tried to *enrol* at the school. A noisy, angry crowd of white people met them there and tried to make them go home. In the end President *Eisenhower* had to send in soldiers to protect the black students so that they could attend the school.

The "Little Rock Nine", now middle-aged men and women, went back to Central High in September 1997 to celebrate the 40th *anniversary* of this turning point for the American civil rights movement. They were happy as they climbed the steps to Central High, with no angry whites blocking the way. Indeed, President Clinton himself was at the door to greet them as they entered.

Much has changed since 1957, in Little Rock and throughout the US. Central High now has its third black principal, and the majority of the students are black. The atmosphere among black and white students is said to be friendly and relaxed.

However, not everything is perfect in the school. More white students achieve high levels in academic subjects, while *remedial classes* are mainly attended by blacks. In exams, whites do twice as well as blacks.

This is not the result of *segregation* and discrimination, but of the poorer backgrounds of the black kids. White kids from well-educated families get a better start in life. The separation according to race continues outside the classroom; at break times, for example, blacks usually sit together, and whites stay with their white friends.

In spite of this, Little Rock is better integrated than many other schools across the whole US. Statistics show that there was a period of success, but many schools are now becoming more segregated again, because many whites have left the big cities for wealthier, more peaceful suburbs, leaving a higher number of blacks at inner-city schools. (392 words)

Fragen zum Text

1 Answer the following questions in complete sentences.
Keep to the information given in the text.

a) Why was the world watching Little Rock in 1957? **(3 Punkte)**

b) Why was the US President there forty years later? **(2 Punkte)**

c) What is life in school like for black students today? **(3 Punkte)**

2 Give your opinion on a student's comment about school:
"We are enjoying ourselves, and it seems to be a good preparation for life." **(4 Punkte)**

Teil B Übersetzung

Wortangaben zu Teil B

troubled .... full of problems
boarded up .... covered with boards
to deteriorate .... here: verkommen

Text

Each year a million people visit Washington to see the White House and the other fine buildings of the capital, but they are not aware that there is another, more *troubled* aspect of the city which should make America ashamed.

Unemployment is high, health care poor and drugs and violent crime are an increasing problem in Washington, where many of the run-down houses are empty and *boarded up*. The city is short of money to provide better living conditions in the poorer areas. The city government is accused of spending too much money on the wrong things in the past, when the economic situation was easier. Roads and bridges were allowed to *deteriorate*, while money was invested to create thousands of new jobs in the city's administration. (127 words)

Teil A Erweiterte Hörverstehensaufgabe

1 Notizen

a) – schools in Arkansas were refusing to integrate
- Central High in Little Rock had no black pupils
- nine black teenagers decided that had to change
- tried to enrol at Central High
- an angry crowd tried to make them go home
- President Eisenhower had to send in soldiers to protect them

b) – in 1997, the "Little Rock Nine" celebrated the 40th anniversary of this event
- were happy when they climbed the steps
- no angry whites blocking the way
- President Clinton himself greeted them at the door

c) – today integration of blacks has improved:
  - third black principal
  - majority of black students at Central High
  - friendly and relaxed atmosphere
  - but: white students → high levels of academic subjects
    blacks → remedial classes
- reasons: poorer backgrounds of black kids
- separation outside the classroom
- today in the USA: new segregation: whites move to wealthier suburbs

Ausführung

a) Although the Supreme Court decided to **admit** black students **in** all public schools in 1954, **a few** schools in Arkansas **were still refusing** to integrate. Central High in Little Rock, **for example, had no black pupils.** Therefore, in 1957, nine black teenagers decided **that had to change.** They tried to enrol at the school, **but** an angry crowd **tried to make them go home.** Because of this President Eisenhower **had to send in soldiers** to protect them. **The whole world** watched this struggle against racism.

W allow ... into
W several
W had still failed
W for instance; W remained all-white
W to change that
W but were met by ... who wanted them to
W called in the army
W The eyes of the world

b) In 1997, the "Little Rock Nine" celebrated the 40th anniversary of this **event**. This time they were happy, **when** they climbed the steps to the school, because **no whites blocked their way.** President Clinton, himself, **greeted them at the door.**

W incident (D Ereignis)
W as
W there were no whites shouting angrily at them
W opened the door for them to enter

c) Today the **integration** of black students **has improved** at Central High. The school has its third black **principal** and the majority of students are black. **The atmosphere between** black and white students **seems to be friendly and relaxed.**
But equal opportunities **have not yet been achieved.** More white students **get high levels** in academic subjects, **while** blacks mainly **attend** remedial classes. In exams **whites do twice as well as blacks.**
This development is not caused by discrimination but by the poorer **backgrounds** of the black kids. However, separation by race **continues outside the classroom,** e.g. at break times.
Today, **across** the USA, a new kind of segregation is **developing**. White families have **started to move to** the wealthier suburbs, **so that** the inner-city schools **are mainly** attended by blacks.

W position
W is much better
W (BE) headteacher
W relations among ... are said to be
W to show no signs of hostility
W are still not open to all
W are taught at a higher level
W whereas; W nicht "to visit" (→ p. 40); W blacks do only half as well as whites.
W This is not the result of ... but of ...
W lifestyles
W goes on; W after classes
W throughout/all over
W growing/increasing
W left the big cities for
W leaving ... to be
W predominantly

Lösungen

WORTFELD: besuchen

to visit	a) offiziell besuchen *(The doctor visits his patients.)* b) besichtigen *(I would like to visit New York.)*
to pay sb a visit	jmdm. (formell) einen Besuch abstatten *(He paid his employer a visit.)*
to go/come and see	freundschaftlich besuchen *(Come and see me at any time you like.)*
to call on	einen kurzen Besuch machen *(I'll call on you as soon as I can.)*
to attend	besuchen (teilnehmen an) *(to attend a high school, lectures, a meeting, church)*
to frequent	regelmäßig oder häufig besuchen *(to frequent a hotel, the seaside, a theatre)*

2 *Comment* – Notizen

Einleitung

personal opinion: partly positive about the student's comment

Hauptteil

a) first part of statement
   pros
   - carefree atmosphere, sheltered period of life
   - sense of community among students, mutual understanding, close contacts

   cons
   - unpleasant experiences, school failure, conflicts, fights, bullying, outsiders

b) second part of statement
   pros
   - a good all-round education
   - general knowledge

   cons
   - knowledge too theoretical, lack of practical skills and technical programmes

Schluss

mixed feelings about student's comment school not all fun and games
educational methods and goals should be adjusted to the 21st century

Ausführung

I largely agree with the first part of the student's **comment** and so do, as far as I know, most of my **schoolmates.**

W opinion/view/statement/evaluation
W friends/pals/chums (D Kumpel, „Spezi")

Most of us think indeed that we are **enjoying ourselves** at school and that the **school days are** the best part of our **lives.** This positive **attitude towards** school is mainly **due to** its comparatively **carefree** atmosphere and the **sense of community** among the students.

W having a great/good time
W times spent at school is
G lives (pl) → p. 24; W response to
W caused by
W light-hearted
W shared identity

Firstly, school time is one of the most **sheltered** periods of life, as youngsters **do not have to make** any serious decisions for their **future** lives. This **helps** the students to **spend** their schooldays without **caring** too much **about** the years **to come.**

W protected
W are not faced with
W prospective; W enables
W go through
W worrying ... about/thinking ... of
W ahead

Furthermore, everyday school life and especially school **trips** or extra-curricular activities **contribute to mutual** understanding and **permit** friendships and even school romances. Thus the student is encouraged to develop a **sense of togetherness** and to **make** contacts with youngsters **with whom (s)he can share** his/her problems, challenges and leisure interests.

W Besides
W outings (D Ausflüge)
W help to develop; W reciprocal
W lead to
W community spirit
W establish
W who share

On the other hand school **also causes** a number of **unpleasant** experiences such as **the pressure of academic achievement** and bad marks, school failure, **conflicts** with teachers and tensions within the **group**, e.g. **fights** in the schoolyard or, more recently,

W is also the reason for
W disagreeable
W hard work
W clashes
W the peer group; W violence

bullying. Frequently students who are **not so popular** are **ignored** by the others and **become outsiders.** But these cases, however unpleasant they are, are **exceptions.**

W harassment (D Mobbing)
W not accepted/rejected; W excluded
W are isolated
W rare

With regard to the second part of the quotation that school seems to be a good preparation for life I do not **entirely** agree. **It is true that** we get a good all-round education, but **isn't** this general knowledge sometimes too **theoretical, unimportant** or even **superfluous?** I firmly believe that more **emphasis** should be **placed** on **practical** skills and on technical **programmes** (e.g. modern technology). These will prepare us better to **come to terms with** the **problems** of the modern world that we will have to **face** in the near future.

W Regarding
W completely
W Certainly
W don't you think ... is
W abstract
W trivial; W unnecessary
W time ... spent
W real-life
W subjects
W to handle; W demands
W solve

All things considered, I **have mixed feelings** about the student's positive comment. **I partly agree with it**, but I **think that it is** somewhat too optimistic and **onesided**. School is not **all** fun and games, but also means hard work and **includes** negative personal experiences of **many a** student. The educational methods and **goals** show **weaknesses** and should be adjusted to the **21st century**.

W All in all; W am in two minds
W agree with it up to a point
W consider it
W biased; W only
W consists of
D many a + Sg.: manch ein
W aims; W defects/imperfections
W new millennium

Teil B Übersetzung

Jedes Jahr besuchen eine Million Menschen Washington, um das Weiße Haus und die anderen schönen Gebäude der Hauptstadt zu sehen, aber sie sind sich dessen nicht bewusst, dass es eine andere, beunruhigendere Seite der Stadt gibt, die Amerika beschämen sollte.

Die Arbeitslosigkeit ist hoch, die Gesundheitsfürsorge mangelhaft und Drogenkonsum und Gewaltverbrechen sind ein immer größer werdendes Problem in Washington, wo viele der heruntergekommenen Häuser leer stehen und mit Brettern vernagelt sind. Der Stadt fehlt es an Geld, um für bessere Lebensbedingungen in den ärmeren Vierteln zu sorgen. Man wirft den städtischen Behörden vor, in der Vergangenheit zu viel Geld für die falschen Dinge ausgegeben zu haben, als die wirtschaftliche Situation besser war. Straßen und Brücken ließ man verkommen, während man Geld für die Schaffung von Tausenden neuer Arbeitsplätze in der Stadtverwaltung investierte.

Anmerkungen

Zeile

2 *fine:* prächtig/prachtvoll/großartig

2 *they are not aware:* sie sind sich nicht im Klaren darüber/wissen nicht

3 *more troubled:* alarmierendere/problematischere

3 *aspect:* Anblick

3 *which should make America ashamed:* deren sich/über die sich Amerika schämen sollte

4 *unemployment:* im D mit Artikel

4 *health care:* das Gesundheitswesen (ebenfalls mit best. Artikel)

4 *poor:* schlecht/unterentwickelt/ärmlich/dürftig

4 *drugs:* Drogen

4 *violent crime:* hier ist im D. keine adjekivische Wiedergabe von *violent* im Sinne „gewaltsam/gewalttätig" möglich; vgl. auch *violent criminal:* Gewaltverbrecher

6 *The city is short of money:* Der Stadt fehlt das Geld/mangelt es an Geld

6 *to provide:* schaffen

7 *The city government is accused:* die Passivkonstruktion im D besser mit „man" + Aktiv zu übersetzen; im D kaum übersetzbar, da es bei uns andere Gremien wie Bürgermeister, Stadtrat oder Stadtverwaltung gibt.

7 *accused: (to accuse sb of sth)* man klagt an/beschuldigt/hält vor

7 *spending:* wegen der Zeitbestimmung *in the past* ist im D nur die Übersetzung im Infinitiv Perfekt „*ausgegeben* zu haben" möglich;
Merke: *to spend on* – ausgeben für; *to spend (time)* – verbringen

9 *easier:* hier keine wörtliche Übersetzung möglich; vgl. auch: *to feel easier:* sich besser fühlen

9 *were allowed:* neben dem wörtlichen „erlauben" hat *to allow* viele Nebenbedeutungen, je nach Kontext, u.a. auch „lassen", vgl. *you must allow the soup to get cold*: du musst die Suppe abkühlen lassen

10 *to create:* natürlich ist auch eine Übersetzung mit Infinitiv möglich: „um ... zu schaffen"

Klassenarbeit 4

Teil A Erweiterte Hörverstehensaufgabe

Wortangaben zu Teil A

to transmit .... to send
interior .... central area (of a country)
amazed .... surprised
to draw to a close .... to draw to an end, to finish
obstacle .... Hindernis

Text

Imagine living in a world which had none of the present-day transportation and communication systems that we take for granted. There would be no cars, lorries, railways, aircraft or ships to transport people and products from place to place. The telephone and the fax machine would not *transmit* messages, and there would be no radio to listen to or television to watch. If you can imagine such a world, you will begin to understand how isolated the colonists in the New World were.

The early settlers stayed close to the Atlantic coast of their new country. Supplies, visitors, mail – all usually travelled by water. Overland movement in this wilderness was almost impossible. The narrow paths made by Indians or by wild animals were the only "roads". Little by little, determined settlers improved these paths so that their ox carts and wagons could use them, and new trails began to open up the *interior* of the country. Mail was carried overland on horseback. America's system of transportation and communication was beginning to develop.

During the 18th century, settlers paddled their small boats along the country's rivers and lakes, and if a colonist could afford it he made his journeys by coach. Communication between the colonies was gradually improving. Newspapers helped to make the ordinary people more aware of the government, and more critical of it. The printing press became an important weapon in America's struggle for independence.

Then, during the 19th century, the rapid growth of the young republic *amazed* the world. A great system of river transportation grew up, using the recently invented steamboat, while fast American ships crosses the oceans. The railroad became more and more important, helping to develop civilization as it bound the continent together with steel. The telephone and telegraph were invented, linking the various parts of the expanding country to create unity.

As the 20th century *draws to a close,* distance is no longer an *obstacle* to travel. The car, airliner and diesel engine have "reduced" the size of the American continent considerably. Radio, movies, television and communication satellites have helped to draw distant regions closer together and to overcome the differences between them. Within hours, today's American can travel by jet between cities that once were months apart, or he can get in touch directly with a foreign country. Modern American life, economy and politics depend on highly developed systems of transportation and communication. (401 words)

Fragen zum Text

1 Answer the following questions in complete sentences.
Keep to the information given in the text.

a) Describe the situation of transportation and communication in early America. How was it developed by the settlers? **(3 Punkte)**

b) In what ways were transportation and communication improved in the 18th and 19th centuries? What important effects resulted from this? **(3 Punkte)**

c) Characterize the developments in the 20th century. **(3 Punkte)**

2 Describe how personal experience, television, and school have influenced your view of the United States? **(3 Punkte)**

Teil B Übersetzung

Wortangaben zu Teil B

decade .... period of ten years
family ties .... familiäre Bindungen
flaw .... Mangel

Text

Throughout the nation's history, most Americans have seen the public school system as a great educational opportunity. No institution has done more to develop equality of opportunity in American society. Recent *decades*, however, point to the danger that if Americans expect too much from their public schools, they may receive too little. People have probably placed more responsibilities on the public schools than these can possibly handle. They are, for example, expected to help harmonize social differences and solve student problems that result from the weakening of *family ties*.

In spite of these dangers, public education is likely to remain one of the most important institutions in American society. Although it has many *flaws*, no acceptable substitute for it has yet been found. (123 words)

Teil A Erweiterte Hörverstehensaufgabe

1 Notizen

a) early America:
- none of the present-day transportation and communication systems (cars ...)
- colonists were isolated
- supplies etc. by water
- overland movement almost impossible
- narrow paths by Indians and wild animals were the only roads

development by settlers:
- settlers improved paths for ox carts and wagons
- new trails opened up the interior of the country
- mail carried on horseback

b) transportation and communication improved

18th century:
- settlers paddled small boats along rivers and lakes
- or made journeys by coach
- improving communication: newspapers, printing press

19th century:
- rapid growth of the country
- system of river transportation (steamboat)
- railroad very important
  - effect: helped to develop civilization and bound continent together
- invention of telephone and telegraph
  - effect: linked various parts of the country to create unity

c) 20th century:
- modern American life depends on highly developed systems of transportation and communication
- distance no longer obstacle to travel
- size of continent reduced by the airliner ...
- distant regions drawn together and differences overcome
- travel by jet within hours
- directly in touch with foreign countries

Ausführung

a) In early America **settlers** didn't have any **of the present-day** transportation and communication systems such as **cars, railways** or ships. **Therefore** they were very isolated.	W colonists W of today's/of the modern W AE automobiles, railroads; W For this reason
As travel overland was almost impossible, **supplies travelled** by water. The only roads were narrow **paths made by** Indians and wild animals.	W provisions; W were transported W tracks; G by (Passiv: von)
But **little by little** determined settlers **improved these paths** so that their ox carts and wagons **could use** them.	W gradually/step by step W made the paths wider W could/would travel on them
Moreover new trails opened up **the interior of the country** and mail could be **carried** on horseback.	W the country's inland part W transported
b) During the 18th century communication between the colonies improved. The settlers began **to paddle** their boats along the **country's rivers and lakes** or, sometimes, **made their journeys** by coach. The printing press and newspapers helped to improve the communication system.	W to move/maneuver W inland waterways W travelled
In the 19th century the country grew rapidly. Steamboats helped **to create** a great system of river transportation.	W Rapid growth characterized the 19th century W to build up
The railroad developed civilization **by binding** the continent together. And **the invention** of the telegraph and the telephone **linked the various parts of the country to create unity.**	G by + Gerund (D indem ...) W with the invention of ... the country was drawn further together

Lösungen

c) **Modern American life depends** on highly developed transport and communication systems. This means	G Kein Artikel; W is based on
that distance is no longer an **obstacle**	W hindrance/barrier
to travel. The **size** of the American	W vastness/dimensions
continent **has been "reduced"** by	G present perfect; W diminished
cars and **airliners**. The use of radio,	W aircraft, air(o)planes
television, and satellite has helped **to**	W to link/connect
draw distant **regions closer together** and to overcome the differences between them. People can travel by jet in a few hours between cities	W areas
which are thousands of miles **apart**,	W away/from there
or they can **get in touch directly** with	W communicate instantly
someone **in a foreign country**.	W abroad

WORTFELD: Reise

journey (größere) Landreise
(to go on a journey, to make a journey, a journey through the USA)

travel a) Singular: das Reisen *(distance is no longer an obstacle to travel)*
b) Plural: große Reise (in ferne Länder) *(Gulliver's travels)*

voyage See- oder Luftreise *(a voyage to America, an ocean voyage by air)*

tour große Rundreise *(to go on a business tour)*

trip a) Vergnügungsreise, Ausflug
(a day trip to the country, a trip to London)
b) zweckgebundene oder regelmäßige Reise
(to make a trip to the doctor's, a business trip abroad)

2 *Comment* – Notizen

Einleitung
views about America
not based on personal experience

Hauptteil
conflicting views about America
a) rather positive picture of America on television: big houses, huge cars, young men, pretty girls, fun
b) more critical picture of the USA in schools: poverty, unemployment, racial discrimination of minorities, crime, drugs

Persönliche Stellungnahme
- both presentations have formed my view
- helped to overcome one-sided picture of America

Ausführung

My **views** about America **are** not **based on** personal experience, as I **do not know** any Americans and have never been to the States. So I do not know if **these are** true or not.	W opinion ... is; W founded on/formed by; W have not met W my opinion is
Television and school **present conflicting** views of America. On television the picture of the U.S. is rather positive. The country seems to be a place where "big is beautiful". The characters **normally live** in enormous houses or in **high-rise buildings**. They generally drive huge cars, too. American **series often** show young, handsome men and **slim**, pretty girls on the beach having fun, surfing, playing or skateboarding.	W show W opposing/contrasting G Adverb vor Verb D Hochhäuser G series/pl series; W frequently W slender
In contrast to this, school has **taught** me that there are problems in the U.S., **for example poverty**, unemployment, homelessness, racial discrimination of minorities, crime and **drug abuse**. However, these are **rarely** shown on T.V.	W as opposed to this; G to teach, taught, taught W e.g./for instance; G ohne Artikel D Drogenmissbrauch W seldom

In think that both **presentations** of the States have **formed** my view. Television has **probably** influenced my opinion of the U.S. the most, **especially** in my childhood, but school has helped me to understand that this view is **onesided** and to realize that I must **be critical about this.**

W descriptions
W moulded/shaped
W almost certainly
W in particular

W biased/partial
W adopt a more critical attitude about this

Teil B Übersetzung

Während der gesamten Geschichte ihrer Nation haben die meisten Amerikaner das staatliche Schulsystem als eine große Bildungschance angesehen. Keine Einrichtung hat mehr für die Entwicklung der Chancengleichheit in der amerikanischen Gesellschaft getan. Die letzten Jahrzehnte weisen jedoch auf die Gefahr hin, dass, wenn die Amerikaner zu viel von ihren staatlichen Schulen erwarten, sie vielleicht zu wenig erhalten. Die Menschen haben den staatlichen Schulen wahrscheinlich mehr Verantwortung auferlegt, als diese möglicherweise verkraften können.
Sie sollen zum Beispiel dazu beitragen, gesellschaftliche Unterschiede auszugleichen und Schülerprobleme zu lösen, die von der Schwächung der familären Bindungen herrühren.

Trotz dieser Gefahren wird die staatliche Erziehung wahrscheinlich eine der wichtigsten Einrichtungen der amerikanischen Gesellschaft bleiben. Obwohl sie viele Mängel hat, hat man bis jetzt keinen annehmbaren Ersatz dafür gefunden.

Anmerkungen

Zeile	
1	*Throughout ...:* Die gesamte Geschichte ... hindurch
1	*nation's: ihrer Nation* (Possessivpronomen zur Verdeutlichung des Bezugs)
1	*public:* öffentlich
2	*educational opportunity:* Bildungsmöglichkeit, Bildungschance
2	*institution:* Institution, Anstalt
3	*... to develop:* auch wörtlicher möglich: *hat mehr getan, um die ... zu fördern*
6	*responsibilities:* Plural im D nicht möglich
6	*to handle:* fertig werden mit, behandeln
6/7	*They are expected to do sth:* wörtlicher: *Von ihnen wird erwartet, dass/Man rechnet damit, dass sie*
7	*harmonize:* in Einklang bringen, *noun: harmony*
8	*result from:* sich ergeben aus
8	*weakening:* Abnahme/Lockerung/(Ab)Schwächung

10 *American society:* im E ohne best. Artikel, im D mit

11 *acceptable:* passend, annehmbar

RECHTSCHREIBUNG: Die Schreibung *al-* und *all-*

Vergleiche:

al-			all-		
almighty	–	allmächtig	*all-powerful*	–	allmächtig
almost	–	fast, beinahe	*all-round*	–	vielseitig
already	–	schon	*all-important*	–	außerordentlich wichtig
alright (adj)	–	in Ordnung	*all right (adv)*	–	in Ordnung
also	–	auch			
although	–	obwohl, obgleich			

Beachte:
Wenn *all* mit einem neuen Wort zusammenwächst, dann fällt ein „*l*" weg.

Klassenarbeit 5

Teil A Erweiterte Hörverstehensaufgabe

Wortangaben zu Teil A

Thomas Jefferson .... American President
to prevent sb from doing sth .... abhalten von
in full swing .... at its height
rural .... opposite of "urban"
to prosper .... to grow
freight .... goods transported by lorries etc
exodus .... when there is an exodus a lot of people leave a place together

Text

The early settlers in the United States were mainly farmers who believed that the traditional values of the country – honesty, hard work, independence – had their roots in simple farm life. Big cities, many Americans thought, were dangerous not only for those people who were unfortunate enough to live in them, but for the nation as a whole. In 1800 *Thomas Jefferson* declared that big cities were dangerous "to the morals ... and the liberties of men".

But not even one of the Founding Fathers could *prevent* the cities in the United States *from* growing. By the 1850s the Industrial Revolution was in *full swing*, and America was well on its way to becoming an urban nation. Millions of people moved into the cities – *rural* Americans, former slaves, and masses of immigrants from all parts of Europe and elsewhere. Cities developed and became wealthy all over the country, but it was the cities of the Northeast and the Midwest – New York City, Boston, Detroit, Chicago and many others – that dominated America's economic and cultural life.

All these cities which *prospered* during the late 19th century had important factors in common. They were all near rivers or seaports, which were necessary for *freight* transport, and each dominated the market in one or two industries: steel in Pittsburgh, cars in Detroit for example.

But from the 1950s onwards these cities began to face problems. Many rich, middle-class citizens, most of them white, began to move out from the city centres to the newly established suburbs, which were safer and quieter. In the late 1960s this movement became a mass *exodus*. Racial tensions, which had been growing for a long time, broke out in cities all over the country. Blacks who had been left behind in the inner cities were no longer willing to tolerate prejudice and poverty. They attacked their own neighbourhoods, burning apartment houses and robbing stores. These riots frightened many of the remaining white people, and so the cities lost many of their wealthier citizens.

In the 1970s, competition from countries such as Japan and Germany became a serious problem for America's industries. To save money companies left town. Many firms moved to other parts of the county where taxes and wages were lower – often to the southern cities of America's "Sun Belt". (381 words)

Fragen zum Text

1 Answer the following questions in complete sentences.
Keep to the information given in the text.

a) What did 19th century Americans think of the big cities? **(2 Punkte)**

b) Describe the development of the big cities in the late 19th century. **(4 Punkte)**

c) What problems were the big cities confronted with after 1950? **(3 Punkte)**

2 State your opinion on the following question: What problems would you have to face if you had to move to the United States? **(3 Punkte)**

Teil B Übersetzung

Wortangaben zu Teil B

graduation .... Abschluss
research .... here: wissenschaftliche Untersuchungen

Text

"Nobody cared if I stayed in school or not." That is the explanation most American secondary-school dropouts give. To deal with this situation, U.S. schools are experimenting with some fresh answers to the age-old problem of students leaving before *graduation*.

Teachers traditionally have concentrated on what is wrong with the students. They have made many efforts to encourage them to remain in school. Now they are looking more at how schools themselves must change and what can be done to stop students from dropping out.

Research has shown that a student failing in first, second or third grade will likely fail again and may finally drop out. Schools will have to seek new strategies for children at an earlier age so that they can experience some successes rather than failure after failure. (129 words)

Teil A Erweiterte Hörverstehensaufgabe

1 Notizen

a) – big cities dangerous for people and for the nation as a whole
- Thomas Jefferson: cities dangerous to the morals and liberties of men

b) – after the Industrial Revolution America became an urban nation
- millions of people moved into the cities (rural Americans, former slaves, masses of European immigrants)
- cities developed and became wealthy: especially in the Northeast and the Midwest (e.g. New York, Chicago etc.)
- prospering cities were near rivers or seaports (freight transport) and dominated the market in important industries (e.g. steel in Pittsburgh)

c) 1950s
- white middle-class citizens moved to safer and quieter suburbs

1960s
- mass exodus from city centres
- racial tensions in inner cities
- Blacks did not tolerate prejudice and poverty anymore and attacked own neighbourhoods
- riots frightened remaining white people and cities lost many wealthier citizens

1970s
- foreign competition (Japan, Germany) became a serious problem for America's industries
- to save money companies left town and moved to other parts of the country (lower taxes and wages)

Ausführung

a) The Americans of the 19th century thought that big cities **were** dangerous for the people who lived	G Zeitenfolge/Indirekte Rede (nicht: would be)
there and for America **as a whole**.	W in them; W altogether
According to Thomas Jefferson they	D laut T.J./T.J. zufolge
were dangerous to America's morals and the liberty of men.	W endangered America's morals

b) After the Industrial Revolution America **became** an urban nation. Millions of people **such as** rural Americans, **former** slaves and **masses** of European immigrants, **moved into** the cities. **All over the country** cities developed and became wealthy, **especially** in the Northeast (e.g. New York) and the Midwest (e.g. Chicago). All these **prospering** cities were near rivers or seaports which were necessary **for freight transport**. And **each** dominated the market in important industries (e.g. steel in Pittsburgh).

W developed into/turned into
W including
W freed; W a great deal of/crowds of; W came to
W Throughout the country
W in particular
W growing/flourishing
W to transport and distribute goods
G each (jede(r) aus einer bestimmten Anzahl)

c) In the **1950s rich** and middle-class, **mainly** white citizens moved from the cities to the safer, **quieter** suburbs.

W/R 1950's; W wealthy
W predominantly
W more peaceful

In the 1960s **this movement became a mass exodus** as racial **tensions broke** out. The Blacks in the city centres were **not willing to tolerate** prejudice and poverty anymore and attacked their own neighbourhoods. These **riots frightened the remaining** Whites. And so the cities **lost** almost all their **wealthier citizens**.

W many more people left the inner cities; W conflicts
G break, broke, broken
W to put up with/accept/were fed up with
W violent disturbances
W made many of the white people flee/leave/go away; G lose, lost, lost; W well-to-do residents

Later, in the 1970s, foreign competition from countries like Japan and Germany became a serious problem for America's industries. In order **to save money** companies **left town** and **moved to other parts of the country where taxes and wages were lower**.

W to cut costs; W left the cities
W went to parts of the country which had lower taxes and wages

WORTFAMILIE: morals

moral	moralisch, sittlich, tugendhaft *(moral standards)*
moral	*(lesson / message)* Moral einer Geschichte, Fabel *(the moral of a tale, to draw a moral from sth)*
morals	*(principles)* Moral(vorstellung) *(Americas morals and liberties of men, his morals are different from mine)*
morale	*(feeling of confidence and optimism)* Kampf-, Arbeitsmoral, Stimmung *(the morale of a team)*
morality	*(ethics, moral system)* Sittenlehre
to moralize	*(to preach)* moralisieren, predigen, sich entrüsten *(to moralize about the dangers of drink)*

2 *Comment* – Notizen

Einleitung

difficult situation, many problems

Hauptteil

general problems:

- loneliness, new surroundings, differences in lifestyle

particular problems:

- at school new subjects
- language difficulties
- cultural barriers
- racial problems, violence, crime

Schluss

not easy to adjust oneself, but maybe positive experience

Ausführung

I think that it would be very difficult to **move to** the U.S. because you would **face** many problems. **To begin with** you would not **know anyone** and so you could be very **lonely**. It might also take some time **to get used to** the new **surroundings** and find your way around.

W to settle in
W be confronted with; W First of all/Firstly; W have any friends
W lonesome
W to get accustomed to
W place where you live/environment

As a rule life in America is very different from the German **way of life**. In school you **would have to** learn new **subjects** and probably have to learn new things even in the subjects you studied in Germany.

G generally speaking
G life in A (kein Artikel); W life-style
G to have to: Ersatzverb zu *must*
D Schulfächer

Besides you may experience language **difficulties** and cultural **barriers** and you may **be confronted with** racial problems, violence and **crime**.

W Furthermore
W problems; W obstacles
W be faced with/have to cope with
G crime (kein pl)

To sum up we can say that it would **certainly** not be very easy **to adjust oneself** to the new country, but **maybe** it would also be a **positive** personal experience.

W In conclusion
W definitely; W to adapt oneself
W perhaps
W rewarding

Teil B Übersetzung

„Niemand kümmerte es, ob ich auf der Schule blieb oder nicht." Dies ist die Erklärung, die die meisten amerikanischen Schüler geben, die die weiterführende Schule abbrechen. Um mit dieser Situation fertig zu werden, versuchen es amerikanische Schulen mit einigen neuen Antworten auf das uralte Problem, dass Schüler vor dem Abschluss die Schule verlassen.

Lehrer haben sich traditionsgemäß auf das beschränkt, was bei den Schülern falsch ist. Sie haben große Anstrengungen unternommen, um sie zu ermutigen, weiterhin auf der Schule zu bleiben. Jetzt schauen sie mehr darauf, wie die Schulen selbst sich verändern müssen und was getan werden kann, um Schüler davon abzuhalten die Schule abzubrechen.

Wissenschaftliche Untersuchungen haben gezeigt, dass ein Schüler, der in der ersten, zweiten oder dritten Klasse vesagt, wahrscheinlich wieder versagen wird und vielleicht die Schule schließlich vorzeitig verlässt. Die Schulen werden neue Strategien für Kinder einer früheren Altersstufe suchen müssen, so dass diese einige Erfolge erfahren können, anstatt laufend zu versagen.

Anmerkungen

Zeile

1 *Nobody ...:* Keiner machte sich Gedanken: allen war es gleich, ob ...

1/2 *explanation most ... dropouts give:* ausgelassenes Relativpronomen *which* nach *explanation* beachten

2 *dropouts:* die die ... Schule vorzeitig verlassen

2 *to deal with:* in den Griff bekommen, zurechtkommen

3 *answers to:* Lösungen des ... Problems

4 *students:* hier nicht *Studenten*, da es um *secondary schools* geht

5 *concentrated on what ...:* stilistisch besser wäre es, ein Verb hinzuzufügen *beschränkt zu untersuchen, was ...*

6 *made many efforts:* waren sehr bemüht, machten sich große Mühe

6 *to remain in school:* weiterhin zur Schule zu gehen

8 *to stop:* davon abhalten

8 *to stop students from dropping out:* englisches *gerund* nach Präposition im D durch Infinitiv *abzubrechen* übersetzen

9 *a Student failing: present participle* durch Relativsatz im D wiedergeben: *ein Schüler, der versagt*

10 *seek:* sich einfallen lassen

11 *strategies:* Taktiken

11/12 *can experience some successes:* einige Erfolgserlebnisse haben können

12 *rather than failure after failure:* als ein ständiges Versagen zu erfahren/als ein Versagen nach dem anderen zu erfahren

Klassenarbeit 6

Teil A Erweiterte Hörverstehensaufgabe

Wortangaben zu Teil A

to retrain .... here: fortbilden
Greek .... from Greece
Korean .... from Korea

Text

In former times most immigrants to the United States came from Europe. For the last 25 years, however, immigration from Asian and Latin American countries to the United States has increased sharply. Nevertheless life in the U.S. disappoints many of those immigrants. They find that the American Dream shown on T.V. and the success stories they heard at home do not give a true picture of the country. The harsh reality of their daily life means to work long hours in low paid jobs just to survive.

But the biggest problems new minority groups such as Asian and Latin American immigrants have to face are the conflicts with the old minorities. Many blacks, for example, feel that they, rather than immigrants, should profit from the money spent by the city in *their* neighbourhoods.

Besides, the newcomers are often criticised for not trying harder to learn English. But their long daily working hours leave them little time to do it. And if there is enough time they will find that waiting lists for English courses are quite long.

But immigrants do not only have problems, they also cause a few problems especially in cities. In New York's schools, for example, language has become a serious problem. Over 100,000 children have difficulties with English. Therefore they are often taught history, maths and science in their own language. At the same time they continue their English language training. Many teachers are being *retrained* to tell pupils about different cultures in their lessons.

However, it wouldn't be right to say that immigrants have caused only problems for New York. Many of them have become much needed young workers. They have also supported the city's economy by opening thousands of new shops and small businesses such as coffee shops which are mostly owned by *Greeks*. *Koreans* run a lot of greengroceries, Mexicans deliver the pizzas, and many Arabs own the newsstands.

Immigrants also have a positive influence on American politics. As they come from almost every part of the world, they will protest when there is a crisis in their homeland and make sure that American citizens and politicians take notice. Thus they are not only learning about the American way of life, they are also teaching Americans about the countries they come from. (376 words)

Fragen zum Text

1 Answer the following questions in complete sentences.
Keep to the information given in the text.

a) Why are some of the new immigrants disappointed by life in the U.S.? **(3 Punkte)**

b) How is teaching at New York's schools influenced by immigration? **(3 Punkte)**

c) What are the positive effects the newcomers have on New York's economy and society? **(3 Punkte)**

2 State your opinion on the following question:
One of the most important aims of education is to increase international understanding. What can schools do to achieve it? **(3 Punkte)**

Teil B Übersetzung

Wortangaben zu Teil B

in terms of .... in Bezug auf
heritage .... Erbe
challenge .... Herausforderung

Text

Today, most of the basic ideals and beliefs of the American people remain those of an earlier America. Yet, both the United States and the world have experienced significant changes since the beginnings of the Industrial Revolution. Throughout much of their history, the American people considered their nation to be a young, growing nation. They knew that it was a relatively poor nation *in terms of* economic power and culture when compared with the nations of Europe.

At the same time, however, the American people were proud of their *heritage* and of the new society they were building. They were confident that through progress, growth and the development of American technology they would meet the *challenges* which faced them. (119 words)

Teil A Erweiterte Hörverstehensaufgabe

1 Notizen

a) – American Dream and success stories not true
– reality: hard work and low paid jobs
– biggest problems: social and cultural ones
– conflicts with old minorities (e.g. Blacks)
– their English not good enough
– little time and long waiting lists for English courses

b) – retraining of teachers
– serious language problems of more than 100,000 children
– teaching of history maths and science in students' own languages

c) – positive economic effects: young workers and new businesses
– influence American political life in times of crisis in their homeland
– immigrants do not only learn about the U.S., they also teach Americans about their countries

Ausführung

a) Some **newcomers** to the U.S. are disappointed **by** life there. They **suddenly** realize that the picture of the "American Dream" as it is **shown on T.V.** and all the stories of success they **heard** at home are not true. Many immigrants must work long hours in **badly paid** jobs just in order to live.

W new arrivals
G by: durch (Passiv)
G Adverb vor Verb
W presented
D im Fernsehen: on T.V.
G to hear, heard, heard
G bad: Adverb badly, aber: low paid
G to pay, paid, paid

Moreover they experience social and cultural problems, **for example** conflicts with old minorities such as the **Blacks** who badly need money and help.

W furthermore
W for instance/F "par exemple"
G the Blacks – the Whites mit pl-s

Often newcomers are also **criticized for** not **trying** to improve their English. **However**, because of their jobs, they often **do not have** the time and **there are not enough places** in English **courses** anyway.	G to be criticized for + gerund W But G Verneinung von *to have* mit *to do* W courses in English are booked up
b) In New York's schools, teachers are being retrained so that they can **teach** their pupils about different cultures.	G to teach (taught, taught) sb about sth
On the other hand immigrant children have serious problems with English. Therefore they often have to be **separated** for **major** subjects such as **maths**, history and science so that they can be taught in their own language.	R separated; W main W maths, math: beide Formen richtig
These children, **numbering** over 100,000 at the moment, also take extra English classes to **help** them learn the language.	G present participle für *who are numbering* G to help sb (to) do sth
c) Immigrants have brought **badly** needed young workers to New York as well as thousands of new businesses. They **own**, for example, coffee shops, greengroceries, pizzerias and newsstands.	W urgently W possess
On the cultural side, immigrants come from all over the world. Therefore, whenever there is a **crisis**, there is always someone to protest and **make** Americans and their politicians take notice.	W crisis – pl crises W to make sb do sth: jmdn veranlassen etwas zu tun

Thus immigrants are not only learning about the U.S., but the Americans are also learning about the **immigrants' homelands**.

W therefore

G Genitiv Plural
W countries of origin

WORTFAMILIE: Politik

politician	Politiker
political	politisch *political parties, political asylum*
politics	Politik (als Wissenschaft) *to study politics*
politic	adj (taktisch) klug, diplomatisch *It would be politic to study this book.*
policy	Politik (konkret) *foreign policy, home policy, government policy*
policy	*e.g. insurance policy* – Versicherungspolice

2 *Comment*– Notizen

Einleitung

important role of schools in international understanding

Hauptteil

a) certain subjects at school (e. g. languages, history, geography favour (AE: favor) an interest in foreign culture
b) personal contact with foreign countries (foreign students, school trips, exchanges)

Schluss

schools provide different opportunities for increasing international knowledge and understanding

Ausführung

Schools can play a very important **role** in **increasing** international understanding. By teaching such subjects as languages, world religions, history, geography and music, children can learn what has **influenced** other cultures and the ways in which they think and act. This will make children aware that **life does exist** outside the city or area where they **live** and not just on television.	W part W promoting/encouraging/enhancing/cultivating W affected G does exist (Betonung) W to live: leben, life – lives: das Leben
In order to make this teaching even more **"real"**, schools could invite foreign guests or members of guests or members of minority groups to speak or organize **educational school trips** and encourage international friendships. Today a lot of schools even have regular **exchanges** with partner schools **abroad**.	W genuine/authentic W class outings/excursions W exchange visits in foreign countries/overseas
Whatever way schools **choose**, the fact that they are providing the **opportunities** to learn about different **lands** and their **peoples** is bound to increase international knowledge and, therefore, understanding.	G to choose, chose, chosen W chances/possibilities W countries D peoples (Völker)

Teil B Übersetzung

Heute sind die meisten der grundlegenden Ideale und Überzeugungen des amerikanischen Volkes diejenigen eines früheren Amerikas. Jedoch haben sowohl die Vereinigten Staaten als auch die Welt bedeutende Veränderungen seit den Anfängen der Industriellen Revolution durchgemacht. Einen großen Teil seiner Geschichte hindurch betrachtete das amerikanische Volk seine Nation als eine junge, wachsende Nation. Es wusste, dass es in Bezug auf Wirtschaftsmacht und Kultur eine verhältnismäßig arme Nation war, wenn man sie mit den europäischen Nationen verglich.

Gleichzeitig war das amerikanische Volk jedoch stolz auf sein Erbe und auf die neue Gesellschaft, die es im Begriff war aufzubauen. Es vertraute darauf, dass es durch Fortschritt, Wachstum und die Entwicklung der amerikanischen Technologie die Herausforderungen bestehen würde, mit denen es konfrontiert war.

Anmerkungen

Zeile

1 *beliefs:* Glaubensgrundsätze

1 *people:* hier: *Volk;* im Folgenden *they* mit Singular *es* übersetzen

1 *to remain:* wörtlich *bleiben;* hier: *identisch sein, entsprechen*

2 *yet:* drückt am Satzanfang den Gegensatz aus *doch*

2 *both ... and:* nicht mit *beide(s)* übersetzen, sondern mit *sowohl ... als auch* oder *wie auch* übersetzen

4 *throughout:* während

5 *relatively:* relativ

6 *compared with:* verglichen mit, im Vergleich zu

8 *however:* drückt am Satzanfang oder zwischen Kommata einen Gegensatz aus (jedoch), kann also nicht mit *wie auch immer* übersetzt werden; Gegenbeispiel: *however* + Adjektiv = wie ... auch immer, z. B. *however late he is*: wie spät er auch immer dran ist

9 *they were building:* bei der Übersetzung ist das *past progressive* zu berücksichtigen: *dabei sein, gerade etwas tun*

10/11 *to meet the challenges:* den Herausforderungen gewachsen sein

11 *to face:* sich etw gegenübersehen, gegenüberstehen

Klassenarbeit 7

Teil A Erweiterte Hörverstehensaufgabe

Wortangaben zu Teil A

Paul Cuffe ... proper name
New Bedford ... proper name
Massachusetts ... proper name
vessel ... ship, large boat
cargoes ... goods
to and fro ... hin und her (back and forth)
salary ... the money sb earns
Sierra Leone ... African state

Text

An Outstanding Black American

Paul Cuffe was born near *New Bedford, Massachusetts,* in 1759, the child of free parents. Like many boys he loved the sea, and he became a sailor before the age of 20. He longed to own a vessel so, with his own hands, he built a small sailing ship. Later he became the owner of several ships, the largest of which was the Alpha. This ship, with its allblack crew, carried *cargoes to and fro between* America and countries in Europe. In time Paul Cuffe became a rich man by the standards of his time, but he wanted to be more than just a successful shipowner.

When he was only nineteen years old, he and his brother went to court to get the right to vote. He explained that he paid taxes, so as a taxpayer he should have the right to vote. He lost his case, but his action made people aware that free Blacks were not allowed to vote. Five years later, in 1783, Massachusetts passed a law to give free Blacks the right to vote.

At that time there were no schools for black children in New Bedford, and Blacks were not allowed to attend schools for white children. Paul Cuffe knew from his own experience how important education was, so he had a school built on his own farm, employed a teacher and paid the *salary* himself. Then he invited all the black children in New Bedford to attend his school.

In the early nineteenth century many people believed that the free Blacks would have a better life if they left the United States and started their own colony in Africa. Most Blacks were opposed to this idea of colonization, feeling that the U.S.A. was their own country and that the problems they faced there could be solved. The idea of a free colony in Africa, however, appealed to Paul Cuffe. In 1811 he sailed to *Sierra Leone*, a small country on the western coast of Africa, where he took steps to found a colony called the Friendly Society for American Negroes. In 1815 he took the first colonists to Sierra Leone in one of his own ships. However, he died in 1817, and by this time few people were still enthusiastic about colonization.

To this day Paul Cuffe is regarded as the first successful black businessman who used his own money and time to try to solve some of the problems of the Negroes. (413 words)

Fragen zum Text

1 Answer the following questions in complete sentences.
Keep to the information given in the text

a) Who was Paul Cuffe and how did he become a rich man? **(3 Punkte)**

b) How did Paul Cuffe improve the living conditions of free Blacks in the U.S.A.? **(3 Punkte)**

c) What was Paul Cuffe's project in Sierra Leone like? **(3 Punkte)**

2 State your opinion on the following question:
Is the United States still a land of opportunity for immigrants? **(3 Punkte)**

Teil B Übersetzung

Wortangaben zu Teil B

extent .... degree
to establish .... to found
to ensure .... to make sure

Text

The earliest settlers who came to the American continent wanted to escape the controls placed on their lives by kings and governments, priests and churches, noblemen and aristocrats in Europe. To a great *extent*, they succeeded. In 1776 the British settlers declared their independence from England and *established* a new nation, the United States of America. In so doing, they overthrew the king of England and declared that the power to govern would lie in the hands of the people. In 1789, when they wrote the Constitution for their new nation, they separated church and state.

This greatly limited the power of the church. Also, they forbade all titles of nobility to *ensure* that there would be no ruling class of noblemen in their new nation. (127 words)

Teil A Erweiterte Hörverstehensaufgabe

1 Notizen

a)
- a black American from New Bedford, Massachusetts, child of free parents
- became a sailor, built a small sailing ship, later the owner of several ships
- the largest ship (the Alpha) had a black crew
- carried cargoes from America to Europe
- became a rich man for his time

b)
- went to court to get the right to vote as a taxpayer
- lost the case, but five years later free Blacks got voting rights in Massachusetts
- no schools for black children
- could not go to white schools
- had a school built on his farm
- paid the salary for a teacher
- invited all black children to his school

c)
- better life for Blacks in a free colony in Africa
- sailed to Sierra Leone in 1811
- took steps to found a colony, the Friendly Society for American Negroes
- took first colonists to Sierra Leone, but then died in 1817
- people no longer enthusiastic about colonization.

Ausführung

a) Paul Cuffe, a black American,	
was born near New Bedford,	W was born of free parents
Massachusetts in 1759, **the child of**	
free parents. He became a sailor but	
he dreamed of being a shipowner. He	
built his own sailing ship and **later**	G to build, built, built
became the owner of several ships.	W in time, eventually
His largest ship, the Alpha, **with its**	W manned by a black crew
black crew, carried goods between	W transported
European countries and America. Paul	
Cuffe became a **rich** man for his time.	W wealthy

b) Paul Cuffe **went to court** when he was 19. He **explained** that as a taxpayer he should have the right **to vote**.	*G* to go **to** court W pointed out/argued W to vote (nicht: to choose)
Although he lost his case, his action made people **aware** that free **Blacks** were not allowed to vote. In 1783, Massachusetts gave free Blacks voting rights.	W realize *G* Blacks, Whites pl-s
Paul Cuffe also knew the **importance** of education, but there were no schools for black children in New Bedford and they **could not** go to white schools. So Cuffe **had** a school **built** on his farm, **employed** a teacher, paid the salary himself and invited all black children **to attend his school**.	W significance W were not allowed to *G* to have sth done: etw machen lassen; W hired W nicht *to visit*
c) In 1811 Paul Cuffe sailed to Sierra Leone because he was **interested in** the **idea** of a free colony in Africa for black Americans. **Once there** he **took steps to found** a colony called the Friendly Society for American Negroes.	*G* to be interested **in** W plan/project W when he arrived W made arrangements W to found, founded, founded (gründen), **aber:** to find, found, found (finden)
In 1815, he took the first colonists to Sierra Leone. However, when Cuffe died in 1817, only a few people were still **enthusiastic about** colonization.	W fond of/interested in

2 *Comment* – Notizen

Einleitung

U.S. still a land of opportunity today, but not as in former times

Hauptteil

a) in the past land of unlimited opportunities, streets paved with gold, "anything goes"

b) – today possibilities no longer unlimited because of economic recession, unemployment
   – but many immigrants still believe in America as the "Promised Land" and in success through hard work

Schluss
in my opinion America even today a land of opportunity; still today many firmly believe in success

Ausführung

In my opinion the United States still **is** a land of opportunity though not like it once was. **In former times** people believed that America's streets were **paved with** gold. For them the U.S. was a country where **"anything goes"** and, therefore, there were many opportunities to **accomplish** anything you wanted. **In recent times** the immigrant situation has become more difficult as the U.S. **has been hit** by economic **recession** and **unemployment**. In spite of this thousands of immigrants continue **to pour into** the country, legally and illegally. They think that America is still the "Promised Land" and that hard work is the key to success.

In **my opinion** the U.S. will remain a land of opportunity as long as people **believe in** America and in themselves.

G Nach the *United States* Verb immer im sg!
W Formerly
W covered with
W everything can happen
W to achieve/to reach
W In the last few years
W has suffered from
W an economic crisis and
W a lack of working places/of jobs
W to come in great masses into
W To my mind/In my view
W to believe **in** sth/sb: an etw/jmdn glauben, aber: the **belief** in: der Glaube an

WORTFAMILIE: Wirtschaft

economic	wirtschaftlich (*economic union:* Wirtschaftsunion)
economical	sparsam (*economical housekeeper:* sparsame Haushälterin)
economically	adv: wirtschaftlich, sparsam
economy	a) Wirtschaft (*the state of the economy:* Wirtschaftslage) b) Sparsamkeit (*economy class:* Touristenklasse)
economics	Volkswirtschaft

Teil B Übersetzung

Die frühesten Siedler, die auf den nordamerikanischen Kontinent kamen, wollten der Kontrolle entgehen, unter die sie Könige und Regierungen, Priester und Kirchen, Adlige und Aristokraten in Europa stellten. Sie waren in hohem Maß erfolgreich. Im Jahre 1776 erklärten die britischen Siedler ihre Unabhängigkeit von England und gründeten einen neuen Staat, die Vereinigten Staaten von Amerika. Durch diese Handlung stürzten sie den König von England und erklärten, dass die Regierungsmacht in den Händen des Volkes liege. Im Jahre 1789, als sie die Verfassung für ihre neue Nation schrieben, trennten sie Kirche und Staat.
Dies beschränkte die Macht der Kirche weitgehend. Sie verboten ebenfalls jegliche Adelstitel, um sicherzustellen, dass es keine herrschende Adelsschicht in ihrer neuen Nation geben würde.

Anmerkungen

Zeile	
1	*to escape:* entkommen
2	*controls placed on their lives by …*: verkürzter Relativsatz für *controls which were placed on their lives by …*
2	*controls:* Zwänge/Machtstrukturen/Überwachung
3	*to succeed:* gelingen
5	*in so doing:* dadurch, auf diese Weise
5	*to overthrow, overthrew, overthrown:* zu Fall bringen
7	*people:* hier nur politische Bedeutung *Volk* als Gegensatz zu *king* möglich. Unterscheide außerdem: *the people is* … – das Volk ist … und *people are* … – die Leute sind …
9	*greatly:* stark, erheblich
9	*to forbid, forbade, forbidden:* untersagen
10	*to ensure*: sichergehen, garantieren

Klassenarbeit 8

Teil A Erweiterte Hörverstehensaufgabe

Wortangaben zu Teil A

Jesse Carr .... proper name
to stake out .... to mark
acre .... about half a hectare
coolie .... an unskilled Asian worker
boundary .... border
to maintain .... here: wahren, einhalten
obstacle .... something which stands in the way and prevents action
gap .... opening

Text

"Keep out!" This is the message that *Jesse Carr* had for all new settlers in northern California. He had *staked out* 80,000 *acres* of land for his own. But settlers from the east continued to come along the trail which passed through a corner of his land. Jesse Carr did not expect to be able to stop the westward migration completely, but he came up with a plan to keep his own cattle empire free from newcomers. He decided to have a wall built of natural stone, shoulder-high, which would surround his property completely. In 1875 he sent for three hundred Chinese *coolies* from San Francisco, and the monumental task began. Passing the heavy stones from hand to hand, the Chinese labourers (AE: laborers) slowly built the wall right round the ranch.

In a small way, history was repeating itself. Many centuries earlier, other workmen had built a mighty wall, the Great Wall of China one of the Wonders of the World. Now Carr was creating a Wonder of the West of his own. It was seven years before Jesse Carr was satisfied with the wall. Within his *boundaries* the only law was Jesse Carr's law, which was *maintained* by a police force consisting of his cowboys. They patrolled the ranch day and night, and anyone trying to steal horses or cattle would simply be shot on sight. Jesse Carr had taken the law into his own hands, and for him it represented a dream come true.

But no one man, not even as strong a character as Carr, could resist America's great westward migration for long. Jesse Carr had many enemies, and they began to join forces against him. In Washington D.C. Congress was made aware of Carr's northern California wall which, as far as the law-makers were concerned, formed an *obstacle* to the settlement of the western lands. The days of Carr's private empire were numbered. In 1893 federal officers came to the ranch with orders to break through the wall and open up parts of Carr's land to settlement. Jesse Carr had to watch as the officers broke down parts of the wall, leaving great *gaps* through which the settlers could enter. The last of the great western cattle kings had to accept that there could be no wall high enough to keep out the forces of change. (390 words)

Fragen zum Text

1 Answer the following questions in complete sentences.
Keep to the information given in the text.

a) Who was Jesse Carr and how did he stop new settlers from moving west? **(3 Punkte)**

b) Show how law and order were maintained on Jesse Carr's ranch. **(3 Punkte)**

c) Why did the American government send the federal officers and what did they do? **(2 Punkte)**

2 Discuss Jesse Carr's position and the government's reaction to this.
What can be said in support of both views?
Whose side do you take?
State your opinion. **(4 Punkte)**

Teil B Übersetzung

Wortangaben zu Teil B

supremacy ...... Vorherrschaft
to dim ...... to become darker
sharecropper ...... Farmpächter

Text

When slavery was abolished, in the 1860s, a new world seemed to open for the millions of black Americans. They were now citizens for the first time. But the hopes that came with the end of slavery were soon disappointed. Ideas of white *supremacy* in the South, along with prejudice and discrimination in the North, *dimmed* the bright promise of freedom.

There followed long years of hardship and suffering. Not accepted by many of their white neighbours, in the North as well as in the South, Negro Americans got along as well as they could. Many of them became *sharecroppers*, struggling year in and year out to make the barest living. Others worked for low wages at hard and unpleasant jobs. (120 words)

Teil A Erweiterte Hörverstehensaufgabe

1 Notizen

a) – last of the great western cattle kings
– he staked out 80,000 acres of northern Californian land
– came up with a plan to keep his own cattle empire free from newcomers
– sent for 300 Chinese coolies
– had a shoulder-high wall built round the ranch

b) – within his boundaries the only law was his law
– law maintained by a police force (his cowboys)
– cowboys patrolled day and night
– people trying to steal cattle would simply be shot on sight
– Carr had taken law into his own hands

c) – wall formed an obstacle to the settlement of the western lands
– government sent troops to break through the wall and open Carr's land to settlement
– officers broke down parts of the wall
– no wall high enough to keep out the forces of change

Ausführung

a) Jesse Carr was the **last of the great western cattle kings** who had staked out 80,000 acres of **northern** Californian land for himself. He **came up with a plan** to keep his cattle empire free from newcomers. **That's why** he **sent** for 300 Chinese coolies and **had** a shoulder-high wall **built round** his ranch.

W the last cattle king of the West – cattle (kein pl-s)
W (nicht: north California!)
W made/worked out a plan
W therefore/thus
G to send, sent, sent
W to have sth done: etw bauen lassen
W around

b) **Within** the **boundaries** of Carr's land, the only law was his own maintained by a police force. This	W inside, W borders
consisted of his own cowboys who	W comprised
patrolled day and night and **shot people trying to steal** cattle **on sight**. Jesse Carr had taken the law into his own hands.	R to patrol, patrolled; G to shoot, shot, shot; W thieves; G to steal, stole, stolen; W as soon as they were seen
c) The U.S. government **sent** officers to	G to send, sent, sent
Carr's land because **they** believed that	G government: they
his wall **formed** an obstacle to the	W provided
settlement of the western lands. **They were ordered** to break through the	G persönliches Passiv they received the order
wall **in order to** open up parts of his	D in order to: um zu (Inf)
land to settlement. Carr had to **watch** as parts of his walls came down. He	W Carr could only watch
had **to realize** that no wall could be	W to accept/to admit
high enough **to keep out** the forces of change.	W to stop

WORTFELD: Land

land
a) Land im Gegensatz zum Meer
(to travel by sea and by land)
b) Landbesitz, Grund und Boden
(fruchtbares Land: *fertile land, landowner*)
c) Land als geographischer Begriff
(homeland, dreamland)

country
a) Land als politischer Begriff
(the people, government, boundaries of a country)
auch Vaterland *(home country; Right or wrong, my country!)*
b) Land im Gegensatz zur Stadt
(*to live in the country:* auf dem Land leben, *country life*)

2 *Comment* – Notizen

Einleitung
rights of the individual opposed to the rights of the community

Hauptteil
a) in favour of Carr:
Carr's activities legal at that time (the first to arrive became the owner)

b) against Carr:
tyranny in his cattle empire; in possession of too much land

Persönliche Stellungnahme
U.S. government was right because Carr owned too much land and used unfair means

Ausführung

The **problem to be discussed deals with** the rights of the individual **in contrast to** the rights of the community.	W issue; W in question; W is about W as opposed to/in opposition with
Jesse Carr was partly right because he arrived first on the land that he marked and, therefore, he could **claim it for himself**. This was not **against** the law.	W demand it as the rightful owner W opposed to
However, the U.S. government was against the tyranny which **reigned** within Jesse Carr's **empire** and against the fact that he owned so much land and **refused to let other settlers onto it.**	W ruled W kingdom W denied admission of other settlers
I think that I would **support** the U.S. government more than Jesse Carr because everyone should **obey** the law of the land, **no matter who** they are and how much land they own. **In addition**, it is not fair that he had so much and other people had so little. The only possible way **to put this right** was the use of force by the U.S. government.	W side with/agree with D to obey s.o. – jmdm gehorchen D egal wer W additionally/moreover/furthermore W to rectify this/correct this/to restore justice

Teil B Übersetzung

Als die Sklaverei in den sechziger Jahren des 19. Jahrhunderts abgeschafft wurde, schien sich für die Millionen schwarzer Amerikaner eine neue Welt aufzutun. Nun waren sie zum ersten Mal Staatsbürger. Aber die Hoffnungen, die mit dem Ende der Sklaverei aufkamen, wurden bald zunichte gemacht. Die Vorstellung einer weißen Vorherrschaft im Süden zusammen mit Vorurteilen und Diskriminierung im Norden trübten die vielversprechende Aussicht auf Freiheit.

Es folgten lange Jahre der Mühen und des Leidens. Die amerikanischen Schwarzen, die von vielen ihrer weißen Nachbarn im Norden ebenso wie im Süden nicht akzeptiert wurden, kamen so gut sie konnten zurecht. Viele von ihnen wurden Farmpächter, die jahrein, jahraus darum kämpften, das Notwendigste zum Leben zu verdienen. Andere verrichteten schwierige und unangenehme Arbeiten für einen niedrigen Lohn.

Anmerkungen

Zeile

1 *in the 1860s:* zwischen 1860 und 1870

2 *were ... citizens:* waren ... im Besitz der Staatsbürgerschaft, sie hatten ... Staatsbürgerrechte

3 *(their hopes were) disappointed:* wörtlich: *enttäuscht*, bessere Variante: *zerschlagen*

3 *ideas of*: der Gedanke an

4 *prejudice:* im E meist Singular, im D Plural

4 *discrimination:* deutsche Fremdwortübersetzung hier besser als *Benachteiligung*

5 *to dim:* einen Schatten werfen auf

5 *the bright promise of freedom:* (wörtlich: *das leuchtende Versprechen der Freiheit*) dieser metaphorische Ausdruck muss freier übersetzt werden: die *verheißungsvolle Erwartung der/Hoffnung auf Freiheit*

6 *hardship:* Not, Mühsal

6 *accepted: past participle* auflösen durch Relativsatz; Subjekt *Negro Americans* an Satzanfang stellen;
to accept: Fremdwort *akzeptieren* besser als wörtliche Übersetzung *annehmen*

9 *year in year out:* Jahr für Jahr

9 *wage(s):* im E meist Plural, D *Lohn*, Löhne

10 *jobs:* hier nicht *Arbeitsplätze*

Klassenarbeit 9

Teil A Erweiterte Hörverstehensaufgabe

Wortangaben zu Teil A

Thomas Garrett .... proper name
Pennsylvania .... state in the USA
Quakers .... Christian religious group
Underground Railroad .... secret organisation which helped slaves to escape
Delaware .... state in the USA
captors .... kidnappers
guilty .... having committed a crime
coffin .... box in which a dead person is buried

Text

Thomas Garrett was born in *Pennsylvania* in 1786. His family's ancestors were *Quaker* immigrants, who believed that all men were created equal before God and therefore that slavery should be abolished.

Thomas spent his childhood helping on the family farm. The Garretts believed in hard work, so they had become quite rich, but they still maintained a simple lifestyle. Although they needed servants to run their large household, they treated them with respect and paid them wages, because it was out of the question for *Quakers* to keep slaves.

Thomas Garrett first became involved in the *Underground Railroad* in 1814. Someone had kidnapped a free servant from his household in order to sell her as a slave. Thomas wanted to release her before her *captors* could take her across the border into one of the states where slavery was legal. While he was searching for her, he heard God call him by his name and order him to help runaway slaves. From this moment on he devoted his life to the task. Soon he became recognised as an active member of the Underground Railroad, whose door was always open to runaway slaves.

It did not satisfy him, however, to simply find homes and jobs for these Negroes. Their children needed an education. As no existing school would accept black pupils, Thomas Garrett built two houses and employed Negro and Quaker teachers who could help them to become free black Americans.

In 1848 two slave-owners accused Garrett of allowing thirteen Negroes – including new-born babies – to stay overnight on his farm during a blizzard. The court found him *guilty* of this "crime", and Garrett was fined $8,000, which left him with no money at all. Thomas declared before the court that he had now paid for all the Negroes he would help during the rest of his life.

Two years later Garrett started doing business in *Delaware*, one of the slave states. When a slave-owner told him he would kill him if he ever came south, Thomas answered that he intended to go there soon and that he would pay him a visit. He kept his word, and when he met his enemy he said: "Here I am. You can shoot me if you like." – There was no shooting.

Garrett lived to see the day when slavery was abolished by law. When he died at the age of 85, eight former slaves carried his *coffin*. (406 words)

Fragen zum Text

1 Answer the following questions in complete sentences. Keep to the information given in the text.

a) What does the author tell us about Thomas Garrett's family and their principles of life? **(3 Punkte)**

b) What were the reasons for Thomas Garrett to become an active member of the Underground Railroad? **(2 Punkte)**

c) How did Thomas Garrett get into difficulties with his enemies? **(3 Punkte)**

2 State your opinion on the following question:
What problems do black Americans still have to face today? **(4 Punkte)**

Teil B Übersetzung

Wortangaben zu Teil B

Pilgrim Fathers .... Pilgerväter
unbearable .... intolerable

Text

The colonists who gained their independence were still mainly English in origin. Most of the immigrants of the late 19th century, however, were not brought to America by ideals of the same kind as those which the *Pilgrim Fathers* had. The Irish and the Eastern Europeans in particular sailed to America in order to escape from *unbearable* poverty, and they were looked down upon by the descendants of earlier colonists.

Although the background of the new arrivals was different from that of the old ones, there was still an important element in common among them all. All were rebelling against something they could not tolerate in their countries of origin, and therefore all were prepared to take great risks to build a new life for themselves. (125 words)

Teil A Erweiterte Hörverstehensaufgabe

1 Notizen

a) – born in Pennsylvania in 1786
- his family's ancestors were Quaker immigrants
- they believed that all men were created equal
- slavery should be abolished
- they believed in hard work
- they had become rich, but maintained a simple lifestyle
- they treated servants with respect and paid them wages
- out of the question for Quakers to keep slaves

b) – Garrett became involved in the Underground Railroad in 1814
- someone had kidnapped a free servant from his household to sell her as a slave
- Garrett heard God call him by his name and order him to devote his life helping runaway slaves (to devote – widmen)
- became recognized as an active member of the U.R.
- found homes and jobs for Negroes and built schools for their children

c) – in 1848 two slave-owners accused Garrett of allowing 13 Negroes to stay on his farm
- was found guilty and fined $ 8,000 (without any money)
- he declared he had now paid for all the Negroes he would help during the rest of his life
- two years later he started doing business in Delaware (slave state)
- a slave-owner told him he would kill him if he came south
- Garrett went to Delaware, but there was no shooting

Ausführung

a) Thomas Garrett was born **in Pennsylvania in 1786. His family's ancestors were Quaker immigrants.** They believed that **all men were created equal** and, therefore, that slavery should be abolished.	G Ort vor Zeit W his family were descendants of Quaker immigrants W everyone was equal G Indirekte Rede

The family **believed in hard work** and had become quite **rich**. However, they still **maintained** a simple lifestyle, treated their servants with respect and paid them wages. **It was out of the question for Quakers to keep slaves.**	W worked hard W wealthy/well-off W led W Keeping slaves was unacceptable to Quakers
b) Thomas Garrett became involved in the Underground Railroad in 1814. Someone had **kidnapped** one of his household's free servants to be **sold** as a slave. While he was **searching for** her, he **heard** God call him by his name and order him to help **runaway** slaves. So he became an **active member** of the Underground Railroad. He **found homes and jobs for the Negroes and built schools for black children.**	W caught G to sell, sold, sold G while + past progressive G to hear, heard, heard W fugitive (adj) W supporter W provided the Blacks with homes, jobs and an appropriate education G child/children
c) Garrett **got into difficulties with** his **enemies** because in 1848 two slave-owners accused him of **allowing** thirteen **Negroes to stay** on his farm. He was found guilty by the court and **was fined $8,000**. This left him without any money. But Garrett **declared** that he **had** now **paid** for all the Blacks he **would help** during the rest of his life.	W came into conflict with G enemy/enemies W letting ... stay, G Singular: Negro W had to pay a fine of; G $-Zeichen vor Zahl G Indirekte Rede
Two years later Garrett **started doing** business in Delaware, a **slave** state. A slave-owner even **told him he would kill** him **if he came** south. But there was no shooting when Garrett **met** his enemy in Delaware.	W set up (to set, set, set) W slave-holding state W threatened (drohte) to kill him G Ind. Rede; nach *if* kein *would* G to meet, met, met

GRAMMATIK: Indirekte Rede

Einleitungssatz	Nebensatz
Past Tense *They believed that*	gleichzeitig **Simple Past** *all men were created equal*
Past Tense *Garrett declared that*	vorzeitig **Past Perfect** *he had now paid for …*
Past Tense *A slave owner told him*	nachzeitig **Conditional I** *he would kill him if ..*

2 Comment – Notizen

Einleitung
American Blacks got equal rights during the Civil Rights Movement of the 1960s

Hauptteil
but in practice today they have to face racial discrimination in
- education (bad schools)
- jobs (manual jobs)
- housing
  a) underclass live in slums
  b) problems of middle class Blacks to move to white areas (result: segregation)

Persönliche Stellungnahme:
racial discrimination not yet overcome – will take many more years for people to change their attitudes and to make dream of equality come true

Ausführung

Many laws have been passed during and after the Civil Rights Movement of the 1960s **making** segregation and racial prejudice illegal **and giving**	W which have made ... and ... given
Blacks, and minorities **in general**, equal	W generally speaking/on the whole
rights. However, **in practice**, many of	G aber: to practise
the black population still **have to face**	W are confronted with
racial discrimination. Because of this they are often **at a disadvantage** in their	W are ... underprivileged/ handicapped
education and, later, in the **job-market**.	W labour market/employment market
Therefore many still have to do manual jobs and **are not promoted**. Maybe their	W do not get their promotion
biggest problem, however, is **housing**.	D Unterkunft (ohne Artikel)
The "underclass" still **live** in the slums but even "middle class" Blacks have	G lives (auch möglich)
difficulties. **Fox example**, when they	W for instance
move into a white **area**, the Whites begin	W district/neighbourhood
to move out. This **leads to increased**	W results in; W growing
segregation and **less** understanding.	G little, less, least
In my opinion discrimination is the biggest problem facing the black population in the U.S.A. today because it	W To my mind/In my view
is something which **affects** every **part of**	W influences/has an effect on
life. People's ideas and **attitudes** won't	W field/sphere of life; W views
change **overnight**. Therefore it will take	W very rapidly/immediately
many more years for Martin Luther King's dream of racial equality and equal	W much longer
opportunity **to come true.**	W to become fact/to really happen

Teil B Übersetzung

Die Siedler, die ihre Unabhängigkeit erlangten, waren ihrer Abstammung nach immer noch vorwiegend englisch. Die meisten Einwanderer des späten 19. Jahrhunderts zog es jedoch nicht nach Amerika auf Grund von Idealen, die denen der Pilgerväter entsprachen. Insbesondere Iren und Osteuropäer fuhren nach Amerika, um der unerträglichen Armut zu entkommen und sie wurden von den Nachkommen der früheren Siedler verachtet.

Obwohl sich die Herkunft der Neuankömmlinge von der der früheren Siedler unterschied, gab es immer noch ein wichtiges Element, das allen gemeinsam war. Alle erhoben sich gegen etwas, das sie in ihren Herkunftsländern nicht dulden konnten, und deshalb waren alle bereit, große Risiken auf sich zu nehmen, um für sich ein neues Leben aufzubauen.

Anmerkungen

Zeile

1 *gained their independence:* gewannen ihre Unabhängigkeit

1 *were still mainly English in origin:* stammten immer noch hauptsächlich/vorwiegend aus England

2/3 *Most of the immigrants ...* wörtliche Übersetzung des zweiten Teils des Satzes klingt im D sehr holprig – ... *weil sie die gleichen Ideale wie die Pilgerväter hatten/weil ihre Ideale denen der Pilgerväter glichen*

5 *to escape:* entfliehen

5 *to look down upon:* abfällig/verächtlich betrachten, als minderwertig einstufen/ansehen

7 *background:* Verhältnisse

9 *to rebel against:* Variante: sich auflehnen gegen

9 *to tolerate:* ertragen

Klassenarbeit 10

Teil A Erweiterte Hörverstehensaufgabe

Wortangaben zu Teil A

Cherokee .... Indian tribe
Sequoya .... proper name
Arkansas ['ɑːkənsɔː] .... state in the USA
fur trader .... Pelzhändler
witchcraft .... skill of using magic powers
cabin .... a small house built of wood
to acquire .... here: to get

Text

By the early 1820s, Indians belonging to the *Cherokee* tribe in the southeastern United States had achieved a considerable degree of civilization. They farmed the land. They made their own cloth, and used it for their clothing. They built roads, schools and churches. They had developed a form of government which was based on the system of the United States.

The tribe's most important achievement, however, was the creation of a written form of the Cherokee language. This was developed by a member of the tribe, called *Sequoya*.

Sequoya had been a hunter and *fur trader* until he was seriously injured in a hunting accident. He was uneducated, and he knew no English. But he was an intelligent man, and he had seen how the ability to read, write and print gave the white man a big advantage. Therefore he decided to develop a Cherokee alphabet – a writing system for his own language. But before he could carry out this task, he spent many hours studying English letters in children's reading-books.

Some of his fellow Cherokees were frightened by the unfamiliar symbols that Sequoya was working on, and they thought he used *witchcraft*. They destroyed his cabin and all the papers he had been working with. In order to continue his work, Sequoya was forced to leave Cherokee country and move westward, living among a group of Cherokees who had settled in *Arkansas*.

Twelve years passed before he returned home, bringing a written greeting from the Arkansas Cherokees in their own language. He had created an alphabet. It consisted partly of English letters, but also included some new symbols that had been invented by him. For the first time the Indians north of Mexico had a writing system of their own, not borrowed from the white man. This wonderful achievement brought a great change in Cherokee education, because thousands of Cherokee Indians of all ages soon learned to read and write their own language. The Cherokees also *acquired* a printing press. First, parts of the Bible were printed in Cherokee, and then they began to publish a weekly newspaper.

Later, Sequoya decided to search for a group of Cherokees, who were thought to have moved across the Mississippi river many years before. He wanted to find common elements of speech and grammar among different tribes. He disappeared into unexplored territory and was never heard of again.

(396 words)

Fragen zum Text

1 Answer the following questions in complete sentences.
Keep to the information given in the text.

a) What do we know about the Cherokee tribe's level of civilization in the 1820s? **(2 Punkte)**

b) What are we told about Sequoya himself and why did he decide to invent an alphabet for the Cherokee language? **(2 Punkte)**

c) Describe how Sequoya developed a Cherokee writing system:
- first steps
- difficulties
- final success

(3 Punkte)

d) How did Sequoya's work improve the life of the Cherokees? **(1 Punkt)**

2 "English only – there is no point in learning other foreign languages."
Do you agree with this statement? Give your opinion. **(4 Punkte)**

Teil B Übersetzung

Wortangaben zu Teil B

degree .... *here*: Abschluss

Text

Brian Williams personifies the American dream. One of eight children born into a poor black family in Kansas City, he has climbed the career ladder to the point where now, at 25, he has a university *degree* and runs his own printing company.

But Williams sees problems ahead: "In the face of all the trouble we're having in this country, I'm fairly certain that the great American dream will not become reality for my children as it did for me. There is a real danger that, for the first time, the young people of today may have less opportunity than their parents to improve their way of life."

In a land founded on hope and optimism, hardly anyone now has a positive view of America's future. Serious social problems and an increasing rate of unemployment are worrying signs. (137 words)

Teil A Erweiterte Hörverstehensaufgabe

1 Notizen

a) – farmed land, made their own cloth, used it for their clothing
– built roads, schools and churches
– developed government based on the system of the U.S.

b) – hunter, fur trader (hunting accident)
– uneducated, knew no English, but intelligent
– ability to read, write and print a big advantage for the white man

c) – first steps:
- studied English letters in children's reading-books

– difficulties:
- Cherokees frightened by unfamiliar symbols, thought he used witchcraft, destroyed his cabin und papers
- Sequoya left, moved westward, lived among a group of Cherokees in Arkansas

– final success:
- created an alphabet: it consisted of English letters, but included new symbols invented by Sequoya

– Cherokees learnt to read and write their own language
– acquired a printing press, parts of the Bible printed, published a weekly newspaper

Ausführung

a) The Cherokees **farmed the land, made** their own **cloth** which they used for their **clothing**. They also **built** roads, schools and churches and they developed a form of government **which was based on** the system of the U.S.

W were farmers
W wove (to weave, wove, woven)
D cloth: Tuch – clothes/clothing: Kleidung
G to build, built, built
G based on/modelled on (past participle)

Lösungen

b) Sequoya had been a hunter and fur trader until he was **seriously** injured in a hunting accident.

W badly

He was **uneducated** and **knew no English.** But he was intelligent, and he had **seen** that the ability to read, write and print **gave the white man a big advantage.**

W illiterate/had not gone to school
W did not speak English
W realized
G gave a big advantage to the white man (nachgestelltes indirektes Objekt mit *to*)

c) Sequoya began to study **English letters** in children's reading-books. But some of **his fellow Cherokees** were frightened by the **unfamiliar symbol**s. They **thought** he used witchcraft and **destroyed** his cabin and papers. Therefore Sequoya **was forced** to leave them. He moved westward **and lived** among a group of Cherokees in Arkansas. Years later he returned **with** an alphabet which consisted of English letters but also **included** new symbols **invented by Sequoya himself.**

W written English
W the members of his tribe
W new/strange signs
W believed
W burnt (to burn, burnt, burnt)
W had to
W living (present participle)
W having created
W contained
G (which) Sequoya had invented/developed/created himself (Aktiv)

d) The Cherokees **learnt to read** and write their own language. They **acquired** a printing press, printed parts of the **Bible** and published a weekly newspaper.

G learnt how to read
W got/bought
W Bible (religiöse Begriffe wie *God, Christian* werden großgeschrieben)

GRAMMATIK: Passiv

Textbeispiele

- *This was developed by a member of the tribe.*
- *he was seriously injured*
- *symbols that had been invented by him*
- *parts of the Bible were printed*
- *He was never heard of*

Bildung

Das Passiv wird mit *to be + past participle* gebildet.
Der Urheber der Handlung wird durch *by* angeschlossen.

Bildung

Infinitive Present	*to be developed* entwickelt werden	**Infinitive Past**	*to have been developed* *entwickelt worden sein*
	simple forms		
Present	*it is developed* es wird entwickelt	**Present Perfect**	*it has been developed* *es ist entwickelt worden*
Past	*it was developed* es wurde entwickelt	**Past Perfect**	*it had been developed* es war entwickelt worden
Future I	*it will be developed* es wird entwickelt werden	**Future II**	*it will have been developed* es wird entwickelt worden sein
Conditional I	*it would be developed* es würde entwickelt werden	**Conditional II**	*it would have been developed* es wäre entwickelt worden
	progressive forms		
Present	*it is being developed* es wird (gerade) entwickelt	**Past**	*it was being developed* es wurde (gerade) entwickelt

2 *Comment* – Notizen

Einleitung
the leading language of Europe and the Western World

Hauptteil
pros
- In most fields of work (business world, computer technology, aviation) usefulness of only one international language
- makes communication less complicated and faster

cons:
- important to know other languages to understand the mentality of the native populations and better insight into cultures
- helps to establish contacts
- promotes international understanding and reduces prejudice
- other languages useful for certain jobs, e.g. French for secretarial jobs
- exchange visits with non-English speaking countries

Persönliche Stellungnahme:
personal view:
- learning of more foreign languages no waste of time, but an opportunity to broaden your horizons and to become aware of other people's ways of life

Ausführung

Today English is the **leading** language of Europe and the Western World. In most **fields of work, e.g.** in the business world, in **computer technology** or **aviation**, it is **indeed** better to have **only** one **international** language. The advantage is that in these areas communication becomes **less complicated** and **faster** than if several languages are **used**.

W nowadays; W main/dominating
W areas of life
W for example/for instance
W electronics
W in airports and air-traffic control
W in fact; W merely; W global/world

W more direct/easier
W quicker
W employed

This does not mean, however, that the knowledge of other foreign languages is **unnecessary**. Firstly languages are important to understand the **mentality** of the inhabitants of the **respective countries**. In this way we get a better **insight into** the different cultures **that exist** in the world.	W Yet this does not mean W that you can do without the knowledge of; W a waste of time W the ways of thinking D jeweilig; W of the countries in question; W understanding of G existing (present participle)
To talk to people in their own language may help to **establish personal contacts**. It also **promotes mutual** understanding and may indeed **reduce** cliches and **prejudice**.	W get in touch with them W increases/favours; D gegenseitig W decrease/lessen W discrimination/bias
Other languages are also useful for certain jobs, e.g. French is **required in secretarial and commercial jobs.**	W is essential for communication in the business world
Finally interest in **exchange visits** with non-English speaking countries (**e.g.** France) would diminish if only English **was** spoken.	W twinning links W such as G were (Konjunktiv)
For all these reasons I think that there is a point in learning different foreign languages. It is not only useful but even **indispensable**. It is **an opportunity** to **broaden** your **horizons** and become aware of other people's **ways of life**.	W Therefore/That is why W absolutely necessary; W a chance; D erweitern; W mind W lifestyles

Teil B Übersetzung

Brian Williams verkörpert den amerikanischen Traum. Als eines von acht Kindern, in eine arme schwarze Familie in Kansas City hineingeboren, hat er die Karriereleiter bis zu dem Punkt erklommen, an dem er nun, im Alter von 25 Jahren, einen Universitätsabschluss hat und seine eigene Druckerei betreibt. Aber Brian Williams sieht Probleme auf sich zukommen: „Angesichts all der Sorgen, die wir in diesem Land augenblicklich haben, bin ich ziemlich sicher, dass sich der große amerikanische Traum für meine Kinder nicht so erfüllen wird, wie es bei mir der Fall war.
Es besteht eine wirkliche Gefahr, dass die Jugend von heute zum ersten Mal vielleicht weniger Chancen hat als ihre Eltern, ihre Lebensweise zu verbessern."
In einem Land, das auf Hoffnung und Zuversicht gegründet wurde, hat jetzt kaum

jemand eine positive Meinung über Amerikas Zukunft. Ernsthafte gesellschaftliche Probleme und eine steigende Arbeitslosenquote sind beunruhigende Zeichen.

Anmerkungen

Zeile	
1	*personifies:* personifiziert/ist die Personifizierung des ...
1/2	*one ... born ... Kansas City, he has climbed ...:* die Konstruktion verlangt im D ein zusätzliches „als"
2	*has climbed the career ladder:* ist die Karriereleiter emporgeklettert
4	*ahead:* voraus, für die Zukunft
4	*in the face of:* in Anbetracht, in Hinsicht auf
4	*we're having:* das *present progressive* drückt den gegenwärtigen Vorgang aus; er kann im D am besten mit Ausdrücken wie *gegenwärtig, zur Zeit, augenblicklich wiedergegeben werden*
5	*fairly:* hier: Adverb mit eigener Bedeutung (ziemlich, recht); sonst Adverb zu *fair* im Sinne von *gerecht*
5/6	*will become reality:* Wirklichkeit werden/sich bewahrheiten/sich als wahr herausstellen
6	*There is:* keine wörtliche Übersetzung mit es gibt, da ist!
6	*real:* echte
7	*the young people of today:* die jungen Leute von heute
7	*may:* die Übersetzung mit *vielleicht* ist fast immer die beste Lösung
7	*opportunity:* Aufstiegschancen vgl. auch *equal opportunity:* Chancengleichheit
8	*way of life:* Lebensstandard, -qualität, -stil
9	*In a land founded ...:* verkürzter Relativsatz für *In a land that was founded*
9/10	*positive view of:* optimistische Einstellung in Bezug auf
10	*increasing:* wachsende, zunehmende
11	*worrying signs:* alarmierende Signale

Klassenarbeit 11

Teil A Erweiterte Hörverstehensaufgabe

Wortangaben zu Teil A

whaling .... the activity of hunting whales
naval .... of a navy
merchant .... a person who buys and sells goods
to emerge .... to appear

Text

Soon after the British colonies had been established in North America, it became obvious that there were great differences between them. The settlers from Europe had to create a new way of life suitable for the kind of country they found themselves in.

In New England good farming land was scarce and it was difficult to move further away from the coast, because of mountains and rival French colonies. So the New England settlers turned to fishing, *whaling* and the supply of *naval* stores as the foundation of their prosperity.

Trading with the West Indies, with the French and the Spaniards made New England *merchants* wealthy and powerful, leading many of them to oppose British rule when in later years they found British laws standing in the way of increased trade.

The colonies in the south, however, depended heavily on farming, the most important crops being rice and tobacco. Tobacco in particular was very profitable. Some of the southern planters, who had plenty of land to use, built up huge plantations and lived elegant lives, while negro slaves did the real labour.

The settlers of Virginia and Maryland, and the Puritans of New England, had to struggle long and hard to establish themselves in what had been a wilderness.

Each colony developed a strong spirit of independence, electing a local assembly or council so that many settlers could take part in the government. The rule of England, on the other side of the Atlantic Ocean, was always weak and a long way away.

Once they had survived the early dangers, and the coastal area at least had become well populated, a commercial and cultural life began to *emerge* with newspapers, schools, a postal service and even theatres. By 1750 it was quite possible to enjoy some of the comforts of life that they had left behind in the old world.

The wealthier merchants and planters used their money to build large homes, usually basing their designs and furniture on the English style. They imported books from England to create libraries for their fine houses, although they usually sent their children to be educated in the motherland.

Some Americans, however, did not enjoy the settled life of the coast and felt the loss of freedom that the growing civilization brought with it. They moved westwards into the unsettled areas on the borders of the colonies until they found their path blocked by French settlers. (401 words)

Fragen zum Text

1 Answer the following questions in complete sentences. Keep to the information given in the text.

a) What kind of conditions did the early settlers find in New England and how did they become prosperous? **(3 Punkte)**

b) What did the economy of the southern colonies depend on? **(2 Punkte)**

c) Describe the kind of civilization that emerged after the early dangers had been overcome? **(3 Punkte)**

2 What is your definition for a successful life? State you opinion. **(4 Punkte)**

Teil B Übersetzung

Wortangaben zu Teil B

handout .... support

Text

To what extent has the position of African-Americans improved since Martin Luther King's death 29 years ago? Today, many of the poorest blacks, living in America's run-down inner cities, are still dependent on public *handouts* and have less hope of escape than ever. The most serious problems are in the areas of education, health, unemployment, drugs and violent crime. On the other hand, some blacks have made progress in U.S. society. About one third now consider themselves to be middle-lass and many have acquired homes in the suburbs in order to provide their children with a better education and a safer neighbourhood. Although there has been a considerable growth in the number of black mayors in the country, blacks are still underrepresented in Congress.

(127 words)

Teil A Erweiterte Hörverstehensaufgabe

1 Notizen

a) conditions
- good farming land was scarce
- difficult to move away from the coast because of mountains and rival French colonies
- prosperity
- turned to fishing, whaling, supply of naval stores
- trade (with the West Indies, the French, the Spaniards)

b)
- depended on farming (most important crops: rice and tobacco)
- plenty of land to use (huge plantations, elegant lives of whites)
- real labour done by negro slaves

c) commercial and cultural life emerged (newspapers, schools, a postal service, theatres)
- by 1750 settlers enjoyed comforts of life like in the old world
- large homes with libraries (designs, furniture English style; books from England)
- children educated in the motherland

Ausführung

a) In New England good farming land **was scarce** and it was difficult **to move away from the coast because of** mountains and **rival** French colonies. The settlers **turned to** fishing, whaling and the **supply** of naval stores. Furthermore they traded with the West Indies, the French and **the Spaniards.**	W rare/there was not enough W to move further inland/westwards W as there were/due to G/W Adjektiv/competing W concentrated on W provision W the Spanish
b) It **depended heavily on** farming. The most important crops were rice and **in particular** tobacco. The white planters had plenty of land **to use** and built huge plantations. They lived elegant **lives while negro** slaves did the **real labour.**	W was largely/mainly based on W particularly/especially/above all W available G lives (Plural bei mehreren Bezugspersonen); W whereas; G Negroes (unregelm. Plural); W hard work/physical labour

c) A commercial and cultural life **emerged** with newpapers, schools, a postal service and even **theatres**.	W developed/appeared/made its appearance; R AE: theaters
By 1750 it was possible to **enjoy** some of the **comforts** of life the settlers **had left behind** in the old world. The **wealthier** merchants built **large** homes **with** fine libraries. They based their designs and furniture on the English style and imported books from England.	W indulge in; W luxuries/pleasures; W used to know; W more prosperous; W stately; W and provided/equipped them with
Moreover they sent their children **to be educated to the motherland.**	G Infinitiv Passiv (erzogen werden); W "back home"/to the mother country

WORTFELD: Grenze

boundary — geographische Grenzlinie
A river is a natural boundary.
the boundary of a town, a boundary stone

border — offizielle Landesgrenze und Grenzgebiet
They crossed the border into Mexico.
border population, border dweller (Grenzbewohner), borderland, borderline

frontier
a) offizielle Landesgrenze (= border)
The town is situated on the Mexican frontier
b) (U.S.) Gebiet an der Siedlungsgrenze, unbesiedeltes Land
life at the frontier, frontiersman frontier town (neugegründete Stadt an der Siedlungsgrenze)
c) (bildlich) Neuland, Grenzgebiet
the frontier of space/science/knowledge

limit — (bildlich) Grenze, Punkt, der nicht überschritten werden darf
a limit to his patience, speed limit, the limits of our abilities, off limits (= Betreten verboten)

2 *Comment* – Notizen

Einleitung
today's society characterized by the importance of success in life (e.g. career, fame, material wealth, social position)

Hauptteil
conditions to be successful
- personal background, healthy and close family ties, family and friends you can rely on
- school education, hard work, good qualifications
- useful connections, personal relations
- friendly personality, hard work, self-reliance, faith in yourself, courage

Persönliche Stellungnahme
personal view:
- leading a wealthy life-style important, but more important: persons you love, to be happy in your occupation and free time
- danger of becoming too ambitious

Ausführung

Our **competitive society** is **characterized** by the importance of success in life. To be successful may be **interpreted** as **making a career, becoming famous, acquiring material wealth** or having a high social **position**.	D Leistungsgesellschaft W marked W understood; G to make **a** career W getting to the top; W accumulating (D anhäufen) riches W status
In order to **achieve** this aim a personal background is **essential**. If you have healthy and close family ties and friends **who you can rely on** you will certainly have more opportunity to **do well**. Of course, your future also depends on your school education and good **qualifications**.	W to reach W of great importance/a big advantage W who are willing to support you/… to give you support; W perform well W exam results

Moreover, in a world of **scarce working places** and **rising** unemployment, useful **connections** and personal **relations** are particularly **advantageous**. They will make your start easier.	W decreasing W jobs; W growing W contacts; W links W valuable/profitable
The **qualities most needed** in our society are a **friendly** personality, but **hard work, self-reliance** and **persistence** are also required. That means that you are expected to **have faith in** yourself and that you do not **lose courage** if you **are confronted with difficulties.**	G qualities that are most needed W agreeable/likeable W effort; W self-confidence D Beharrlichkeit; W perseverance W believe in W give up W are faced with/have to deal with/to cope with problems
In my **opinion** the importance of success is that leading a **wealthy** life-style may in itself be a desirable aim, but it is not the only thing that **counts**. It is also essential that there are people you love, that you **are happy in your occupation** and that you retain some **free time** for yourself. If you **are too ambitious** you may have to **sacrifice** too much.	W view W prosperous W matters W have a satisfying/fulfilling job W leisure time; W set your aims too high/are overambitious; W give up/renounce

Teil B Übersetzung

In welchem Maße hat sich die Stellung der Afro-Amerikaner seit dem Tod von Martin Luther King vor 29 Jahren gebessert? Heute hängen viele der ärmsten Schwarzen, die in den heruntergekommenen Innenstädten Amerikas leben, immer noch von öffentlicher Unterstützung ab und die Hoffnung, dem zu entfliehen, ist geringer als je zuvor. Die schwer wiegendsten Probleme findet man in den Bereichen Ausbildung, Gesundheit, Arbeitslosigkeit, Drogen und Gewaltverbrechen. Andererseits sind einige Schwarze in der amerikanischen Gesellschaft vorangekommen. Ungefähr ein Drittel sieht sich jetzt selbst als zur Mittelklasse gehörig an und viele haben in den Vororten Häuser erworben, um ihren Kindern eine bessere Ausbildung und eine sicherere Umgebung zu bieten. Obwohl es eine beträchtliche Zunahme bei der Anzahl schwarzer Bürgermeister im Land gegeben hat, sind die Schwarzen im Kongress immer noch unterrepräsentiert.

Anmerkungen

Zeile

1 *to what extent:* inwieweit, wie sehr, in welchem Ausmaß

2 *today:* heutzutage

2 *living in:* verkürzter Relativsatz für *who live in ...; living* nicht wörtlich mit lebend übersetzen

3 *run-down:* verwahrlost

3 *handouts:* (Geld-)Zuwendungen

4 *of escape: dem zu entkommen;* verbale Übersetzung flüssiger als das wörtliche *der Flucht*

4 *than ever:* denn je

4 *most serious:* ernstesten, größten

5 *education:* Erziehung ist hier im Kontext zu allgemein

5 *crime:* Kriminalität

6 *have made progress:* haben sich emporgearbeitet/sind aufgestiegen; genauer: haben Fortschritte erzielt

7 *middle-class:* Mittelschicht

8 *to provide:* wörtlicher: *zur Verfügung stellen, versorgen mit*

9 *neighbourhood: Nachbarschaft,* besser: *Wohnviertel*

9 *Although there has been a considerable growth in ...:* Obwohl die Anzahl der ... beträchtlich gestiegen ist/zugenommen hat

10 *mayor:* nicht mit *major* (Major) verwechseln

Nützliche Redewendungen für den comment

Einleitung

first of all	zuallererst
to begin with	zunächst einmal
in order to decide	um zu entscheiden,
whether ... or not	ob ... oder ob nicht
to outline the main points	die Hauptpunkte kurz umreißen/skizzieren
firstly – secondly –	erstens – zweitens –
thirdly – finally/lastly	drittens – schließlich
in the first/second/third place	erstens/zweitens/drittens

Aufzählung

as well as	ebenso wie
in addition (to that)	zusätzlich
additionally	zusätzlich
besides	außerdem
moreover	darüber hinaus
furthermore	weiterhin
above all	vor allem

Abwägen von Argumenten

on the one hand ... on the other (hand)	einerseits ... andererseits
we must consider the advantages and disadvantages	wir müssen die Vor- und Nachteile in Betracht ziehen
arguments for and against	Gründe für und wider
to discuss the pros and cons	das Für und Wider diskutieren
compared to/in comparison with	verglichen mit/im Vergleich zu
in theory ... in reality	in der Theorie ... in Wirklichkeit
both ... and	sowohl ... als auch
not only ... but also	nicht nur ... sondern auch
in former times/previously	früher
nowadays/at the moment	heutzutage/im Augenblick

Vergleichen

compared to/in comparison with	verglichen mit/im Vergleich zu
you can make/draw a comparison between ... and ...	man kann einen Vergleich anstellen zwischen ... und ...
to bear comparison	einem Vergleich standhalten
to compare well/badly with ...	bei einem Vergleich gut/schlecht abschneiden

Kontrastieren, Einschränken

however	jedoch
yet	doch
nevertheless	nichtsdestoweniger
whereas	wohingegen
although/even though/though	obwohl
in spite of/despite	trotz
unlike	anders als, im Gegensatz zu
in contrast to/with sth	im Gegensatz zu etw
in/by contrast	im Gegensatz dazu
as opposed to sth	im Gegensatz zu etw
to be in opposition to sb	im Gegensatz zu jmdm stehen
on the contrary	im Gegenteil
sth is contrary to sth	etw steht im Gegensatz zu etw
my attitude is quite opposite to	meine Einstellung ist das genaue Gegenteil dazu

Bezüge herstellen

with reference to	in Bezug auf
with regard to	im Hinblick auf
regarding	hinsichtlich
as regards	was ... betrifft
as far as ... is concerned	soweit es ... betrifft/angeht
concerning	bezüglich

Verallgemeinern

on the whole	insgesamt
in general	im Allgemeinen

as a rule	in der Regel
broadly speaking	allgemein gesprochen
to some extent	in einem gewissen Maß
to a large extent	in hohem Maße
in all respects	in jeder Hinsicht

Erläutern

for example	zum Beispiel
for instance	zum Beispiel
such as	wie zum Beispiel
e.g.	z. B.
in particular	insbesondere
an example of this would be	ein Beispiel dafür wäre
to give you an example of	um Ihnen ein Beispiel dafür zu geben
what I mean	was ich meine
to illustrate this point	um diese Aussage zu veranschaulichen
let me take/cite an example	lassen Sie mich ein Beispiel geben/anführen
to exemplify what I mean	um zu erläutern, was ich meine

Genauere Erklärung

what I mean is	was ich damit meine, ist
what I'm saying is	was ich damit sagen möchte, ist
what I'm trying to say is	was ich damit zu sagen versuche, ist
the point I'm trying to make is	was ich zum Ausdruck bringen möchte, ist
to be more accurate	genauer gesagt

Betonen

I'd like to point out/emphasize that	ich möchte darauf hinweisen, dass
I must stress the point that	ich möchte betonen, dass
to bring sth into prominence	etw herausstellen/in den Vordergrund rücken
I'd like to draw your attention to	ich möchte Ihre Aufmerksamkeit auf ... lenken

Ausnahmen anführen

apart from	abgesehen von
except	ausgenommen
with the exception of	mit Ausnahme von

Einräumen / Zugeben

If you think about it carefully, you must admit that ...	wenn Sie einmal genau darüber nachdenken, müssen Sie zugeben, dass
it is generally admitted that	es wird allgemein zugegeben, dass
there's no denying the fact that	die Tatsache ist nicht zu leugnen, dass
we can't rule out the possibility that	wir können die Möglichkeit nicht ausschließen, dass

Begründen

this is due to/owing to	das rührt von der Tatsache her
because/as/since	weil/da
because of	wegen
the reason for this is	der Grund dafür ist
this can be explained by	das lässt sich dadurch erklären
for the simple reason that	aus dem einfachen Grunde, dass
for one/some reason or (an)other	aus diesem oder jenem Grund
let me explain why	lassen Sie mich erklären, warum
the main/basic reason is	der Hauptgrund dafür ist
and that's the reason why	und deshalb
I have every reason to believe that	ich habe allen Grund zu glauben, dass
there is reason to believe that	es gibt Gründe zu glauben, dass

Folgern

thus	so, auf diese Weise
therefore	deshalb
consequently	folglich
for this reason/(all) these reasons	aus diesem Grund/(all) diesen Gründen
as a result	folglich
so that	sodass

Schluss und Zusammenfassung

eventually, finally	schließlich/zu guter Letzt
last of all	zuallerletzt
last but not least	nicht zuletzt
in conclusion, I would like to	abschließend möchte ich
we can draw the conclusion	wir können den Schluss ziehen
to sum up/to summarize we can say that	zusammenfassend kann man sagen, dass
to cut a long story short	um es kurz zu sagen
all in all	alles in allem
in short/in brief/briefly	kurz gesagt
in a word	mit einem Wort
all things considered	wenn man alles in Betracht zieht
much more could be said in regard to the subject under discussion	es könnte in Bezug auf das zur Diskussion stehende Thema viel mehr gesagt werden

Persönliche Stellungnahme

a) allgemein

I think that	ich glaube, dass
in my opinion/in my view/ to my mind	meiner Meinung/Ansicht nach
my point of view is	mein Standpunkt ist
to be of the opinion that	der Meinung sein, dass
this is a matter of opinion	dies ist Ansichtssache
in my experience	nach meinen Erfahrungen
to advocate (doing) sth	für etw eintreten
as far as I know	soviel ich weiß
as far as I am concerned	was mich betrifft/angeht
to be aware/unaware of a problem	sich eines Problems bewusst/ nicht bewusst sein
personally I believe that	ich persönlich glaube, dass
my point is	was ich sagen/worauf ich hinaus will, ist
my own view of the problem is	meine eigene Ansicht über das Problem ist
I take the view that	ich vertrete die Ansicht, dass
as/the way I see it	wie ich es sehe

to tell the truth	um ehrlich zu sein
the fact is that	Tatsache ist, dass

b) übereinstimmend

I agree entirely/absolutely with	ich stimme mit ... völlig überein
that's exactly my own view	das ist genau meine Meinung
I'm of exactly the same opinion	ich bin genau derselben Meinung
I'm convinced that	ich bin überzeugt, dass
it's quite obvious that	es ist ganz offensichtlich, dass
I firmly believe that	ich glaube fest, dass
I feel something should be done about it	ich meine, es müsse da etwas getan werden
that's just how I feel	ich bin genau derselben Meinung
I agree, and I'd go further and say that	dem stimme ich zu und möchte darüber hinaus noch anfügen, dass
that's perfectly true	das ist vollkommen richtig
I'd like to support this view	ich möchte diese Ansicht stützen

c) nicht übereinstimmend

I partly disagree with	ich bin teilweise anderer Meinung als
I don't entirely agree with	ich stimme nicht völlig überein mit
I agree in principle, but	im Prinzip bin ich derselben Meinung, aber
personally, I wouldn't go as far as that	ich persönlich würde nicht so weit gehen
that's not the way I see it	so sehe ich das nicht
I see things rather differently myself	ich meinerseits bin ziemlich anderer Meinung
I'm not at all convinced that	ich bin keineswegs davon überzeugt, dass
I'm not absolutely sure	ich bin mir keineswegs sicher
I can't say for certain	ich kann nicht mit Gewissheit sagen
it's difficult to say for certain	es ist schwierig mit Gewissheit zu sagen
I find it difficult to reach a conclusion but I'm tempted to say	ich finde es schwierig, eine Schlussfolgerung zu ziehen, aber ich bin versucht zu sagen
I have my doubts as to	ich habe meine Zweifel bezüglich

surely there is some doubt about	sicher besteht ein gewisser Zweifel hinsichtlich
this statement demands qualifying	diese Aussage bedarf einer näheren Erläuterung

Interessen, Pläne, Absichten

to be interested in	Interesse haben an
to show an/some interest in	Interesse zeigen für
... interests me a lot	... interessiert mich sehr
my main/particular interest is	mein besonderes Interesse ist/gilt
my hobby is	mein Hobby ist
I'm a ... fan	ich bin ein leidenschaftlicher ... Anhänger
I go in for	ich interessiere mich für
I have the intention of doing sth	ich habe die Absicht etw zu tun
I firmly intend to do sth	es ist mein fester Entschluss etw zu tun
I am prepared to do sth	ich bin bereit etw zu tun
I am determined to do sth	ich bin entschlossen etw zu tun
I'm planning to do sth	ich habe vor etw zu tun
I'm very keen on doing sth	ich ... leidenschaftlich gern

Interesselosigkeit, Gleichgültigkeit

I find ... rather uninteresting/ boring	ich finde ... ziemlich uninteressant/ langweilig
I don't take any great interest in	ich interessiere mich nicht besonders für
I couldn't care less	das interessiert mich überhaupt nicht
it's all the same to me whether	es ist mir vollkommen gleichgültig, ob
... is a matter of complete indifference to me	... ist mir vollkommen egal
I can't say I find	ich kann nicht behaupten, dass ich
... so very fascinating	... so faszinierend finde
... isn't for me	... ist nichts für mich
... isn't my cup of tea	... ist nicht meine Kragenweite
... means nothing to me	... bedeutet mir nichts

Die wichtigsten Wörter zu den Übersetzungstexten der Zentralen Klassenarbeiten der letzten Jahre

abolition	Abschaffung
to abolish	abschaffen
to absorb	aufnehmen, integrieren
abundance	Überfluss
abundant	reichlich vorhanden
achievement	Leistung
to achieve	erreichen, erzielen
acquisition	Erwerb
to acquire	erwerben
administration	Verwaltung
amount	Menge
apprentice	Lehrling
area	Gebiet, Bereich
to argue	argumentieren, behaupten
to argue over	sich streiten über
to assemble	sich versammeln, zusammenkommen
to attend school	die Schule besuchen
attitude	Haltung
average	Durchschnitt
average	durchschnittlich
to ban	verbieten
to be to do sth	etw tun sollen
boarded up	mit Brettern vernagelt
to boast	prahlen, sich rühmen
both ... and	sowohl als auch
to run a business	ein Geschäft führen
to catch up	aufholen
choice	Wahl
civil service	Staatsdienst
to claim	behaupten

to come to do sth	schließlich etw tun
comparatively	verhältnismäßig, relativ
to have sth in common	etw gemeinsam haben
to complain about	sich beklagen über
consequently	folglich
considerable	beträchtlich
to contain	enthalten
to continue to do sth	weiterhin etw tun
curriculum	Lehrplan
custom	Sitte, Brauch, Gewohnheit
decade	Jahrzehnt
degree	Grad, Maß
to a high degree	in hohem Maß
university degree	Hochschulabschluss
to demand	fordern, verlangen
dependent on	abhängig von
to design	entwerfen
to describe	beschreiben
desperate	verzweifelt, hoffnungslos
determined	entschlossen
discouraged	entmutigt
dissatisfied	unzufrieden
effort	Anstrengung, Bemühung
to encourage	ermutigen, fördern
essential	wesentlich
even(ly)	gleichmäßig, ausgeglichen
expansion	Ausdehnung
to expand	sich ausbreiten, sich ausdehnen
extent	Ausdehnung, Grad, Maß
to a certain extent	in gewissem Maße
to escape (from)	entkommen, entfliehen
to establish	errichten, gründen
exaggerated	übertrieben
failure	Versagen
to fall behind	zurückbleiben

family ties	familiäre Beziehungen
far from (doing sth)	anstatt (etw zu tun)
to feel (that)	glauben, dass
for the most part	größtenteils
forefathers	Vorfahren
foundations	Grundlage
to found	gründen
goal	Ziel
to achieve a goal	ein Ziel erreichen
gradually	allmählich
graduation	Schulabschluss
habit	Gewohnheit
health care	Gesundheitsfürsorge
heated	hitzig, erregt
hostility	Feindschaft
human dignity	Menschenwürde
improvement	Verbesserung
to improve	verbessern
to indicate	hinweisen auf, andeuten
in spite of	trotz
to increase	wachsen, zunehmen
increasingly	zunehmend
indignation	Entrüstung
inferior	minderwertig, unterlegen
to inherit sth	etw erben
instead	anstatt, stattdessen
integration	Eingliederung
to integrate	eingliedern
invention	Erfindung
to invent	erfinden
inventiveness	Erfindergeist
inventive	erfinderisch
issue	Problem, Streitfrage
lack of	Mangel an
literacy	Lese- und Schreibfähigkeit
to be literate	lesen und schreiben können

to be likely to do sth	wahrscheinlich etw tun
to long for	sich sehnen nach
to have a closer look at sth	sich etw genauer ansehen
to look down (up)on sb	auf jmdn herabsehen, jmdn verachten
to look upon sb	jmdn ansehen, betrachten als
magnificent	herrlich, prächtig
mainly	hauptsächlich
majority	Mehrheit
manner	Art, Verhalten
manners	Benehmen, Sitten, Umgangsformen
mayor	Bürgermeister
to meet with resistance	auf Widerstand treffen, stoßen
melting pot	Schmelztiegel
minor	kleiner, geringer, geringfügiger
needs	Bedürfnisse
new arrival	Neuankömmling
newcomer	Neuankömmling
obvious	offensichtlich
opportunity	Gelegenheit, Chance, Möglichkeit
equal opportunities	Chancengleichheit
equality of opportunity	Chancengleichheit
to be opposed to sth	einer Sache ablehnend gegenüberstehen
oppression	Unterdrückung
permission	Erlaubnis
to permit	erlauben
persecution	Verfolgung
to persecute	verfolgen
point of view	Standpunkt
poverty	Armut
predominantly	vorwiegend
prejudice	Vorurteil(e)
pretty (adv)	ziemlich
professions	akademische Berufe
to provide sb with sth	jmdm etw zur Verfügung stellen, besorgen, liefern

public school (U.S.)	öffentliche/staatliche Schule
purpose	Zweck, Ziel, Absicht
to question	ausfragen, befragen
race relations	Rassenbeziehungen
racial tension	Rassenspannungen
readily	bereitwillig, gern
to reduce	verringern
to rely on	sich verlassen auf
reputation (for being)	Ruf (zu sein)
research	Forschung, wissenschaftliche Untersuchung
to resist	sich widersetzen
respect for the law	Achtung vor dem Gesetz
to result from	sich ergeben aus
rightful	rechtmäßig
run-down	heruntergekommen
to secure	sichern, schützen
to seek (sought, sought)	suchen
(racial) segregation	Rassentrennung
self-reliance	Selbstbewusstsein
to share sth with sb	etw mit jmdm teilen
shortage of	Mangel an
skill	Geschick(lichkeit)
skills	Fertigkeiten, Fähigkeiten
solution	Lösung
to solve	lösen
to spend on	ausgeben für
state	Zustand
steadily	fest, ständig, stetig
suburb	Vorort, Vorstadt
suburban area	Vorstadtgebiet
successive	aufeinanderfolgend
to suggest	vorschlagen, hinweisen auf
suicide rate	Selbstmordrate
to be supposed to do sth	etw tun sollen

to be supportive of sb	jmdn unterstützen
to make sure	sich überzeugen, sich vergewissern
to survive	überleben
thanks to	Dank
threat to	Bedrohung für
to threaten	(be)drohen
throughout	überall
treatment	Behandlung
to be unlikely to do sth	wahrscheinlich etw nicht tun
unbearable	unerträglich
value	Wert
very first	allererst
violent crime	Gewaltverbrechen
welfare	Wohlfahrt, Sozialhilfe
within	innerhalb
yet (Satzanfang)	doch

cattle — Rind(vieh)
ranch — Farm mit Tieren

to satisfy (satisfied) — zufriedenstellen, befriedigen

to shoot shot shot — schießen

citizen — Staatsbürger
to suffer — leiden
to struggle — kämpfen